NOT A NOVEL

Also by Jenny Erpenbeck

Jenny Erpenbeck

NOT A NOVEL
A Memoir in Pieces

Translated from the German by Kurt Beals

A NEW DIRECTIONS
PAPERBOOK ORIGINAL

The translation of this work was supported by a grant from the Goethe-Institut, which is funded by the German Ministry of Foreign Affairs.

Manufactured in the United States of America
First published as a New Directions Paperbook (NDP1484) in 2020

Library of Congress Cataloging-in-Publication Data
Names: Erpenbeck, Jenny, 1967- author. | Beals, Kurt, translator.
Title: Not a novel : a memoir in pieces / Jenny Erpenbeck ;
translated from the German by Kurt Beals.
Other titles: Kein Roman. English
Description: New York : A New Directions Book, 2020. |
Originally published in German as Kein Roman. Identifiers: LCCN 2020021691 |
ISBN 9780811229326 (paperback ; acid-free paper) | ISBN 9780811229333 (ebook)
Subjects: LCSH: Erpenbeck, Jenny, 1967- |
Authors, German—21st century—Biography.
Classification: LCC PT2665.R59 Z46 2020 | DDC 833/.92 [B]—dc23
LC record available at https://lccn.loc.gov/2020021691

10 9 8 7 6 5 4 3 2 1

New Directions Books are published for James Laughlin
by New Directions Publishing Corporation
80 Eighth Avenue, New York 10011

For my father

Contents

Preface

Many different eras are collected in this volume.

I remember one summer in a house in the countryside, a house that hasn't been our house for a long time now: I was sitting at the electric typewriter, writing a seminar paper on a fairly obscure topic, but one that had provoked me to intensive reflection and obsessive writing. I hadn't even chosen the topic myself, it was my professor's suggestion. That was the first time that I experienced how someone else could open a door for me into my own reflections. I typed, looked out at the lake, typed some more. Whenever I wanted to change some part of the text, I would take scissors and cut it up into individual paragraphs, shuffle them around on the floor until the collage was just right, and then reach for the glue. A long-forgotten approach to writing, it was 1992, a time we now refer to as "the last century." When my friends came to visit, they left me alone with my work in the morning, in the afternoon we would go for a swim together, cook, talk, lie in the sun. I was in my mid-twenties.

I bought my first computer in 1994 and used it to write my first book, *The Old Child*. When the book came out in 1999, I was living in Austria, working at the opera in Graz, I'd only recently started directing my own productions. After the book was published and the first positive reviews appeared, I started getting requests for short stories. I'd never written a short story. I said yes. Twelve pages seemed like a good length. The desk in my study was so high that I could sit on a bar stool and look straight out the window at an enormous mountain. I sat there between rehearsals and on the weekends and wrote, the vaulted ceiling above me was more than 400 years old, the window opened outward in the typical Renaissance style. My publisher and I collected the stories in a volume that appeared in 2001, my second book.

Now people were asking me if I'd like to write about an East German word that had been forgotten, if perhaps I'd like to write a travelogue, if I'd like to write about what literary associations I had with the word "suction." Yes, I would. Writing was a game in which I encountered myself. I moved back to Berlin. The time that I had for writing now was Monday through Friday from 10 a.m. to 1 p.m.—the hours when the nanny took our son out for a walk. My husband worked in another city. I wrote *The Book of Words*, which appeared in 2004. The solicitations were starting to pile up; this or that journalist, editor, writer, or publisher wanted to know: Would I like to write about my favorite fairy tale? About my literary role models? About what motivates me to write? About my childhood? Or about what music means to me? Of course I would. These projects and ideas, conceived by other people, revealed stories that were waiting within me, brought memories to the surface that were entirely my own. My child was growing up, now my writing hours stretched from 9 a.m. to 3 p.m.—unless I was working on a stage production. Could the kindergarten in Nuremberg find room for an extra child while I was in town for six weeks of rehearsals? I started writing my first longer novel, *Visitation*, which appeared in 2008. That was the same year that my mother died. I received a prize for the book and gave an acceptance speech. The date of the speech fell during my period of mourning.

I received another prize, then another. Often the prizes have names. Names of authors who are familiar, but sometimes other names that aren't familiar. What does this or that author have to do with me? Have I ever read the author's works? I read the author again, or for the first time, I spend three weeks, four weeks, six weeks reading. Browse through my own library. Discover the self I used to be in my old notes and annotations. The genre of the acceptance speech offers a great deal of freedom, except in one respect: When you get the prize, you *have* to give the speech. Is there a new novel on the way? A friend asks me if I'd like to write her a screenplay. Another friend asks if I'd write a text to go with her photos. And do I like the Beatles? An author asks if I'd like to participate in a series of events on the topic "Living and Writing in the Age of Competitive Society." I load and unload the dishwasher, hang the laundry out to dry, bake cakes for my child's birthday. I wonder if the boxes from my mother's apartment will sit in our hallway forever, waiting to be unpacked.

In 2012, my novel *The End of Days* appears. The University of Bamberg invites me to give a series of lectures on poetics. How long is a lecture? 40 to 50 minutes, they say—that's about 20 to 25 pages per lecture. There are supposed to be three lectures. At least half a year of work. Are you writing another novel yet? I go on reading tours to cities in Germany, and also abroad. I pack suitcases. Who will take care of the guinea pigs? What hotel am I staying in, anyway? Am I interested in the topic "Landscapes of Childhood"? Yes, very much so. I receive a prize, and another, and another. The prize money helps me get by. The namesake authors are interesting. I stand at my bookshelf pulling out this or that book, reading this or that passage. The date for the award ceremony is already set. Would I like to tell high school graduates in Saarland what I think is the most important thing in life? That's a hard one. What *is* the most important thing in life? I'm inducted into an academy for the first time, and I'm expected to introduce myself, to say how I became who I am, in roughly five minutes. How *did* I become who I am? In Berlin, an agreement that the minister of the interior had made with African refugees is retroactively annulled. I write the first open letter in my life. To this day, I still haven't received a reply.

In 2015, my novel *Go, Went, Gone* appears. Would you like to describe a landscape painting? Hey, Jenny, I'm editing a volume about "hope," do you want to write something for it? I'm inducted into two more academies, the dates for the induction speeches are already set. I'm a different person in Mainz than I am in Berlin or Darmstadt, that much is clear. Can you write something about the refugee crisis? Would you like to say a few words about Einstein as a refugee? One of the refugees I wrote about dies. I write an obituary. I receive a prize. The date of the award ceremony falls during my period of mourning. Each of the nominees is asked to give a brief speech about his or her favorite book and the significance of reading. Could you write an introduction? For this author, I'm truly happy to. What will the title of your keynote be?

In this collection, I am now looking back, for the first time, at many years of my life, at the thoughts that filled my life from day to day, thoughts assembled in these texts that have led a life of their own, and a life of *my* own, alongside my novels, short stories, and plays. In Berlin I had my desk arranged perpendicular to the window for a while, then I put it back so that I could look out the window again. Outside my window, there are plane trees and lindens. The desk where I sit is my grandfather's desk, which was also my mother's desk for many years after my grandfather died. I keep my paper clips in the same drawer where my mother kept hers. Outside, the voices and shouts of children can be heard from the playground. Now and then a car drives by. When a short text like this is finished, I print it out and fasten it with a paper clip.

JUNE 2018

LIFE

At the Ends of the Earth

There is nothing better for a child than to grow up at the ends of the earth. There's not much traffic there, so the asphalt is free for roller-skating, and parents don't have to worry about any bad guys roaming around. What business would a bad guy have on a dead-end street?

The apartment that we're living in when I'm first old enough to go down to the street on my own is on the third floor of an elegant old building with elegantly crumbling plaster, bay windows, enormous double doors for an entrance, and a wooden staircase, the monstrous head at the end of the banister has been worn to a shine by countless hands. Flora Strasse 2A, Flora Strasse 2A, Flora Strasse 2A. The first words I learn after *mama* and *papa* are this street name and this house number. That way if I ever get lost I can always say where I belong. Flora Strasse 2A. Squatting in the stairwell of that building, I learn how to tie my shoes. Just around the corner, on Wollank Strasse, is the bakery where I'm allowed to go shopping by myself for the first time in my life, at age four or five, when my parents send me down with a shopping bag and the magic coins that they've counted out to buy rolls for breakfast. The bakery has hand-carved wooden shelves and a cash register where the cashier turns a crank before she puts the money in. A bell chimes when the drawer is opened. Wollank Strasse comes to an abrupt end a few hundred meters further down, at a wall. That's the end of the line for bus number 50. My parents don't have to worry about any bad guys roaming around, what business would a bad guy have on a dead-end street? In those days, they send me down to the courtyard to play by myself in the sand, a large fir tree casts its shadow on

3

the sandbox, and when dinner is ready my mother calls down to me from the window. There's a dance school on the second floor of our building, from the courtyard you can hear the tinkling of the piano and the voice of the teacher instructing her students in the steps.

On the other side of the wall, past what I know as the end of Wollank Strasse, the elevated train goes by. It runs to the left and to the right, but neither of those directions is open to us. One station further to the left, but on our own side of the wall, my grandmother lives together with her husband and my great-grandmother in a two-room apartment, in one of those Berlin tenements with one courtyard after another. To reach their apartment you have to go all the way to the third courtyard back from the street. The building is actually on a corner, and if you could enter from the other side, their apartment would be at the front. But since that side has been declared a part of the border strip, the passable part of the street comes to an abrupt end just shy of the corner, at a wall. In this neighborhood, where my grandmother and great-grandmother live in their tenement, it's always winter. When I look at the snowflakes in the greenish glow of the streetlights, I feel dizzy, coal is hauled up from the cellar, the third courtyard is paved with concrete, and the ashcans in the courtyard are always surrounded by puddles or dingy reddish snow. Baths are only taken once a week in this household, since the bathwater has to be heated in a special furnace. The only ventilation for the bathroom comes from a tiny window that can be opened with a metal rod mounted above the toilet, a rod that I believe is infinitely long. It runs the entire length of the ventilation shaft, beginning in the bathroom and continuing across the top of the pantry (which is separated off from the kitchen) until it finally reaches that tiny window, which I never actually see. In the kitchen, there's a big, round glass jug on the floor filled with fermenting grape juice that's supposed to turn into wine, but sometimes it turns into vinegar. On the sideboard I see a canning jar full of the leeches that my grandmother has to apply to herself to prevent thrombosis. When I spoon out the pear compote for dessert, I look uneasily at the leeches and the lids of the jars. My grandmother doesn't wash the dishes under running water, she uses two bowls that she pulls out of the kitchen table like drawers. In my great-grandmother's bedroom, where I sleep too when I spend the night, a lacquered wooden clock with golden numbers ticks throughout my entire childhood. This room, which is never heated, is also where my great-grandmother stores her pepsin wine, and she keeps her knitting inside the compartment of the unused tiled stove. In that same compartment, alongside her knitting, she also lays the pins that she removes from her hair before going to bed, undoing her bun and letting her long, gray braid fall down her back. When I look from the bedroom or the living room down to the street, which isn't a street anymore, I can watch the soldiers on patrol, or count the elevated trains that pass, running left and right. I see the strip of sand, the fluorescent lights, the snowflakes swirling in their green light, then the barricades, the watchtowers, and the wall, behind that the train tracks, behind the train tracks the garden plots, and behind the garden plots an enormous building with many windows, perhaps it's a school, or a barracks. On Sundays, when I come to the tenement house where my grandmother lives with her husband and her mother, it always smells like roast pork, steamed potatoes, and cauliflower; it could be the roast pork, steamed potatoes, and cauliflower that my grandmother has prepared, but it could be from the neighbors. You never know.

Shortly before I start school, we move to Leipziger Strasse 47. A boxy pair of blue-and-white high-rises, ours is 23 stories tall, the one next door is 26; these are the first buildings to be finished along the grand socialist avenue that leads to Potsdamer Platz, at least that's how it would be described today. But during my childhood Leipziger Strasse doesn't lead to Potsdamer Platz, instead it comes to an abrupt end just shy of Potsdamer Platz, at the point where the wall turns a corner. That means that the West is there to the left of our building, and the West is also there further along, where the wall turns the corner, just past the end of the line for bus number 32. I learned about that on Wollank Strasse, in the Berlin neighborhood of Pankow. But there are other things that I didn't learn in Pankow. In Leipziger Strasse, when we move in, there's just the pair of buildings where we live, a supermarket, a school, and two apartment buildings that were seriously damaged in the war, nothing else. In Pankow, I learned to ride a bike in the public park, I fed ducks in the palace gardens, I dragged my feet through the autumn leaves when we went for Sunday strolls in the Schönholzer Heide. Now there's nothing around us but mud. My walk to school leads through the mud of the giant construction site, my walk to the supermarket leads through the mud of the giant construction site, my walk to piano lessons leads through the mud of the giant construction site. In the mud, I find a twenty-mark bill, it's green. If I hadn't found that bill in the mud—a miracle!—I surely would have forgotten by now what a twenty-mark bill looked like back then. Our Sunday strolls take us down the smaller streets that branch off from Friedrich Strasse to the west, since that's the only place with asphalt where I can roller-skate, the asphalt is bright gray and smooth, and we can walk down the middle of the street, since there isn't any traffic there. What business would a driver have on a dead-end street?

The high-rises keep growing and filling up with people, including children who become my friends in school. When my friend in the building across from ours oversleeps, we see the one dark square in the seventh row of windows, between countless little bright squares, and we call to wake her up. The construction of socialism is always tied in my mind to this construction site where I live. To the left of our building is the high-rise that houses the Springer publishing company, but that's on the other side of the wall, as if the wall were a mirror reflecting our evil twin back to us. And further along, near the bend in the wall, roughly across from my schoolyard, the upper half of a building can be seen, its facade displaying not only two glowing cursive letters, *BZ*, but also a glowing clock. Throughout all of my years in school, I read the time for my socialist life from this clock in the other world.

We live on the thirteenth floor. On the thirteenth floor, a child starts to wonder about certain things, for instance, if it would be possible to balance on the balcony railing. I decide against it, for reasons that I no longer remember, but it's a close call. Sometimes, when I forget my key to the apartment and my mother isn't home yet, I stand at the hallway window facing west, passing the time by counting the double-decker buses that come and go from the Springer high-rise. We don't have double-decker buses in the East. From thirteen floors up, I have a good perspective. Depending on the time of day, the buses come every five or ten minutes. One day I set a record, I count 26 buses. At some point we move into a larger apartment, which means moving to the sixth floor. A high-rise that large is like a city unto itself, and changing apartments just means rolling up or down a few floors, from one space to another, hauling the furniture up or down in the elevator. Living on the sixth floor isn't just an advantage from the standpoint of my survival, since the temptation of vertigo isn't so strong, it's also an advantage because when all three elevators are out of service, it doesn't take so long to climb the stairs. Whenever I climb up or leap down the shallow steps of that stairwell with its smell of piss and dust, its walls painted a rusty red, I think of our geography teacher's advice that in case of a nuclear attack we should take shelter in the stairwell near the banister. The nuclear attack never comes while I'm living on Leipziger Strasse, there's only a small earthquake one night—we and many of our neighbors run down the rusty red stairwell with its smell of piss and dust, our sweaters pulled over our nightshirts, all the way to the ground floor, where we stand outside the giant block that has spit us out, looking up at it with concern and considering the possibility that all 23 floors might fall on our heads, but that doesn't happen either.

At the age of thirteen, a child starts to wonder about certain things. For instance, whether both people have to stick their tongues out when they French kiss, or just one person at a time. The ABCs of kissing are recorded on a scrap of paper that's grown crumpled from repeated studying. My school friends and I always bring it with us when we venture into the ruins of the Deutscher Dom on the Gendarmenmarkt, where we discuss the hierarchy of kisses and test out our conclusions with a series of experiments: a kiss on the hand—respect; a kiss on the forehead—admiration; a kiss on the cheek—affection; a kiss on the mouth—love. In these ruins we always have the sky above us. In our dusty clothes we return home to our newly built apartments. As childhood gradually turns into something else, and Leipziger Strasse finally becomes a real street instead of a construction site, we move. My mother has seen enough of these blue-and-white boxes, we move into an old building on Reinhardt Strasse at Albrecht Strasse, diagonally across from the Deutsches Theater. Looking out the window of my childhood bedroom, I now enjoy a stunning view—across the lots that bombs left clear—of old Berlin apartment houses silhouetted against the sunset. The sun still sets in the West. At some point, Reinhardt Strasse comes to an abrupt end at a wall. A hundred meters from our house is the end of the line for bus number 78. Now that I know the ABCs of kissing by heart, a boyfriend takes me to the ruins on Museum Island. A birch tree is growing on the ground level. To get to the second floor, you have to climb the birch and then carefully cross over to the cracked marble floor. Up there, a white Venus stands in front of the burned-out windows of the gallery. There is nothing better for a child than to grow up at the ends of the earth.

MAY 2006

Open Bookkeeping

What are you going to do with my furniture when I'm gone? my mother asks me. Oh, I say, we'll see. It's worth a lot, you can sell it. Let's see what happens, I say. You're attached to it, aren't you? I don't say anything. You know we even changed your diaper on the table here. I don't say anything. But it won't fit in your apartment. No, I say.

It's not going to be easy to sell my apartment, my mother says. Don't be silly, I say. The neighbors have been trying to sell theirs for six months and they still haven't managed. Now they want to rent it out. Ah, I say. It doesn't even make sense, it's really nice here. No, I say, it really doesn't make sense. It'll be quite a hassle for you, my mother says. I don't say anything.

My mother says: We have to go to the bank, you need to be authorized to access my account. I know, I know, I say. It's important, she says. Yes, I know, I say. When do you have time—this Thursday? No, I say, I won't be here on Thursday. Next week, then? Yes, I say. When? my mother asks. I tell her I'll have to look at my calendar first. My mother says: Okay. A few weeks later she tells me: I didn't even need your signature, I just had to give them your name.

So when my mother dies, I'm already authorized to access her account. I can use her account to pay for her funeral and the funeral repast, the gravestone, and the cemetery fees, I can keep paying off the mortgage and the maintenance fees for her apartment, at least in the short term, while I try to sell it, and I can use a small trust that she left me to cover the monthly rent for the storage unit where I've had her furniture moved.

I choose an urn. I choose a spray of flowers. I choose rose

petals to scatter into her grave. I hire a speaker to deliver the speech that I write for my mother. I have her mail forwarded to me. At first the forwarding request can't be processed, because I've forgotten to enter my own name in the "care of" field. An understandable mistake, since the only reason I'm filling out a forwarding request in the first place is that I'm no longer taking *care of* my mother. I have to submit the form a second time, and this time I write my mother's name, *care of* my name. I cancel my mother's subscription to the daily newspaper that she always read while drinking her afternoon tea, I receive a confirmation that the remaining balance of €202.07 will be refunded. The reason given for the cancellation is: deceased. I send my mother's rail discount card back, the railway company refunds €91.66 of the €110 that my mother had paid two and a half months earlier. I have her telephone service cut off and request that her name be removed from the telephone book. Her final bill, the balance for her last phone calls with me, comes to €16.99. I cancel my mother's account with the radio and television fee collection center. "This user's account will be terminated at the end of the month. This user's account has no outstanding balance."

On the morning when my mother is cremated, I spend two hours sitting at home, in front of the window, on the chair where she always sat, waiting for the time to pass.

I cancel my mother's membership in the General German Automobile Association. I write an obituary that appears in the newspaper that she always used to read while drinking her afternoon tea. I receive €170.03 for the obituary.

By the time the tax office inquires what personal property and real property I have inherited—real estate, assets, securities, jewelry, carpets, gold, or silver—6 weeks have passed since my mother's death. "All information regarding the value of the estate should reflect the value on the date of death." But the tax office doesn't want to know if I inherited a half-empty pack of cigarettes, a bathrobe with a used tissue in the pocket, or a bouquet that wasn't even wilted yet. They also don't want to know if I inherited my shoe size, my voice, or the way that I bend over when I put on stockings from my mother. They most certainly don't want to know if I inherited the recipe for meatballs in creamy caper sauce, the straw Christmas tree decorations, or the rummy game with score cards from all the games we played in the past five years, each score written down with the corresponding date. The NS 17 form, which is used to calculate inheritance tax, also doesn't have a column for the 10 bottles of shampoo and 10 tubes of conditioner that I inherited from my mother. My mother bought them all at once in order to get as many golden customer appreciation tokens as possible from the pharmacy and give them to my son, her grandson, to play with. I wash and rinse my hair with that shampoo and conditioner for the next year and a half.

8 weeks after my mother's death, the artists' social security fund sends me a bill for €1.42 for the last day that my mother was alive, since it was the first (and for my mother also the last) day of the month, but none of the employees of the artists' social security fund would want to know that on that day I took the wet pants and the wet shirt that the surgeon cut off of my mother and hung them out to dry on my laundry line, and that I also inherited this way of hanging out laundry from my mother. "The remaining balance is too low to be automatically deducted from your mother's account. Therefore we ask that you transfer this amount to one of the accounts listed below. Please include your mother's insurance number with your payment."

I find a stonecutter who makes very nice gravestones and give him the dates of my mother's birth and death so that he can create a design.

And so I inherit a furnished two-bedroom apartment with 108 square feet of storage space in the basement. I inherit bookcases full of books, cabinets with drawers full of files, photos, and notes, I inherit a storage closet full of bedding, cleaning products, tools, shoes, large pots, an ironing board, a laundry-drying rack, a broom, and a scrub brush, I inherit combs, brushes, makeup, shower gel, and creams, inherit dishes, knives, and forks, bottle openers, inhalers, aspirin, flower vases, paper clips, diskettes, envelopes, I inherit 1 television, 10 stools, 3 tables, 1 bed, 2 sofas, 2 armoires, 1 cabinet, 1 wardrobe, 11 lamps, 1 chandelier, 5 rugs, 1 wicker chest, I inherit winter coats, diaries, records, I inherit 8 bottles of wine and 3 of mineral water, inherit 1 music box, inherit necklaces, rings, and brooches, inherit frozen roasts and frozen zucchini, 2 cans of lentils, 1 half stick of butter, 1 lemon, 3 cups of probiotic yogurt, I inherit 1 bicycle, 1 lawn mower, 1 washing machine, 1 Biedermeier writing desk, 1 wing chair, 2 paintings, 12 framed pictures, 10 apples and a banana, some bread, I inherit pens and white paper, inherit twine, coasters, and potholders, inherit coins and banknotes from every country imaginable, cardboard boxes of buttons and yarn, 1 large and 1 small sewing box, I inherit hundreds of slides and 3 projectors, inherit 8 ashtrays, 3 cartons of cigarettes, 1 old cassette recorder, 2 mirrors, I inherit 1 computer, 1 printer, 2 old laptops, 1 old monitor, extension cords and 1 toaster, I inherit 2 houseplants, several bedspreads, wool blankets, pillows, inherit empty suitcases, inherit handbags and slippers, nutcrackers, Christmas lights, Easter bunnies, Christmas stockings, 2 cartons of Blue Onion porcelain, tablecloths, towels, eyeglasses, I inherit sweaters, stockings, blouses, underwear, inherit cardigans and neck scarves from my mother. I also inherit my own suitcases full of winter clothes that I always kept in my mother's basement in the summer, and my own baby clothes, as well as a small board that I painted when I was in preschool, I inherit 2 boxes of stones that I collected as a child, and my small Chinese parasol.

After half a year has passed, people begin to ask: Are you writing anything new? No, I say, not yet.

6 months after my mother's death, I pay the bill that the insurance company sent for the ambulance that took my mother to die, €30.00. I cancel the insurance policy for my mother's fifteen-year-old car, and give the car to a friend. I hire a real estate agent to handle the sale of my mother's apartment. The maintenance fees and the mortgage for the apartment come to €750 a month. In order for my mother's apartment to be sold, it has to be empty. I start packing boxes. At home, I sort through my own books to make room for my mother's books, papers, and photo albums. That winter, I arrange the first move; two movers bring my mother's desk, a cabinet, and a chest to my apartment. The day of the move is icy, and I'm glad that the men don't slip as they're carrying the heavy furniture.

In January 2009, I learn that the manager of my mother's apartment building has run off with so much money that the electricity and water for the whole complex are about to be shut off. To prevent that from happening, the owners' association votes that all members will make two special payments in addition to the regular maintenance fees, in order to "ensure liquidity."

My mother's apartment is very nice, but no one buys it, probably because it's too deep in the east side of Berlin, in Weissensee, on the road to Moscow. I send an email to about a hundred friends and acquaintances. No one needs an apartment. I wake up at night haunted by fear.

I go to the stonecutter's shop to inspect his design.

My mother's tax advisor asks me to prepare my mother's tax returns for the months of 2008 when she was still alive. I take a linen chest and various boxes out to our cabin in the country. When I've packed my mother's books, some of the boxes go to my apartment, some go to the antiquarian bookstore, some go to the country. In my search for potential buyers for my mother's apartment, I put up flyers at an art academy in Weissensee. None of the professors needs an apartment.

People ask me: Are you writing anything new yet?

In the process of closing my mother's bank account, I realize for the first time that she also had liability insurance. Unfortunately, I am informed, the payments that have been deducted from her bank account for the entire time that she was already dead cannot be refunded. That spring, barely a year after my mother's death, I rent a small truck and hire two students. We take 10 boxes, the bicycle, the lawn mower, and various kitchen utensils to the country. On the drive out and back, we talk about film. That spring, the electric company, which has been providing electricity to my mother's empty apartment for the past nine months, refunds me €119.81. The apartment still costs €750 a month. I decide that if all else fails, I'll rent it out for now, and I place an ad in the paper. Around that time there's some misunderstanding with the phone company, my phone stops working for weeks, and eventually the internet connection goes out, too. My apartment ad appears in the paper, but the phone number that I provided is out of service. In order to sell some lamps, my mother's bed, and her TV console on eBay, I have to sit in an internet café. While I'm there, I also send emails to the doctors in all 8 departments of the hospital in Weissensee, offering them my mother's apartment. None of the doctors needs an apartment.

When an employee at the bank that gave my mother the loan for her apartment hears that I'm planning to rent it out, she advises me that the bank is a public development bank, which means that

I'm not even allowed to rent out the apartment on the open market, that is, I can't charge the normal rent, and I have to receive special permission for each tenant. She advises me to refinance the loan.

I inspect the gravestone. The inscription will be colored in with brown paint.

The next move, early in the summer—this time with a moving company—makes its first drop-off at the storage unit, where I store 1 sofa, 1 cabinet, 3 shelves, 1 armchair, 2 chairs, and some boxes. From the storage unit we proceed to my apartment, where I unload some more boxes, a chest of drawers, and some pictures.

I hire a second real estate agent to handle the sale or rental of the apartment. He advises me to clear out the very last items that are still sitting or lying around, at least to move them down to the basement for now. I should also take down the curtains and then have the apartment painted.

You must be working on a new book by now, aren't you?

Since a self-employed writer would never be able to get a loan in Germany these days, I spend time negotiating with my husband's Austrian bank about refinancing the loan before my son's school lets out for the summer. The loan is approved, with my husband as guarantor.

I clean everything out of my mother's freezer and pull the plug out of the outlet. Now, for the first time, the apartment is completely silent. I take the frozen food that my mother cooked, carry it home in a well-insulated bag, and stash it in my own freezer.

The gravestone is finished now, it's installed in the cemetery. When she finishes her calculations, my mother's tax advisor tells me that my mother is owed a €5 tax refund. My telephone is working again. The internet is working again. On the day in autumn when I finally clean out my mother's apartment once and for all—clean it so thoroughly that not even a bit of thread or crumpled newspaper remains—on that day, when I take my mother's slippers, the scrub brush, the whisk broom, the dust pan, and the toolbox down to the basement, when I carry the ashtray with the last cigarette that my mother ever smoked to my car (later, on the drive back to my apartment, the ashes that my mother tapped into the ashtray will crumble), on that day I run into my mother's neighbors in the hall. When they hear that I'm open to renting out my mother's apartment rather than selling it, they say that they'd be interested. A few weeks later we reach an agreement.

Now I'd like to call my mother.

DECEMBER 2009

The Pressure Cooker

When I'm abroad, where I travel with just 1 suitcase, a change of shoes, and 2 or 3 books, it nearly feels like I'm not missing anything, from that nearly empty distance it's nearly possible for me to forget about my overfilled apartment in Berlin. My apartment was never exactly empty, but now, since my mother's death, it contains two of everything. There are 2 packages of laundry detergent, 4 pairs of boots instead of 2, there are 2 winter coats, 40 travel guides instead of 20, 2 sewing boxes, 2 washbasins, 2 trunks, 2 desks, and so on. My job is to take these two lives that have suddenly been crammed together in my apartment and make them one, but it's not an easy job. My job is to distinguish between those things that reminded my mother of something and those things that remind me of something. To use the things that I can use, and give away the rest, or sell them at the flea market. But since it simply isn't possible to take every single thing that once belonged to one life and attach it to another—whether by putting it to use, giving it away, or selling it at the flea market—it stands to reason that I will also have to throw some things away.

In the basement, I've found the pressure cooker that my mother used throughout my childhood to cook green cabbage stew. Its lid doesn't close anymore, and even if it did, I'd be afraid that the pot would explode, since I don't know much about pressure cookers. So I put it in the box of things to throw away.

The box of things to throw away sits in the trunk of my car for several days, until I have time to throw the things away. The only thing that stays in the box is the pressure cooker. I want to think about taking it to the recycling center, since it's a large pot and there's a lot of metal in it. Again and again, when I open the trunk, I see the silver pot with the red enamel lid sitting there in the dark, I see the whistle on the lid that always whistled when the green cabbage stew was finished (or when the pressure was too high?), I take off the red lid and look into the pot of my childhood. The bottom of the pot is stained a light brown, my mother always washed it by hand.

At some point, after I've been driving around Berlin with the pressure cooker in my trunk for several weeks, I get the idea that I should bury the pot. A quiet burial on our land outside the city, where my son has already buried moles and mice. A very quiet burial, since I don't want anyone to know that I'm the kind of person who holds a funeral for a pressure cooker. How easily the box of things to throw away has transformed itself, in the trunk of my car, into a box of things to take to the country. As I drive out to the country, I tell myself that the pot will always be there under the ground, my silent partner; I consider whether I should fill it with dirt for all eternity, and how deep the grave should be. Does aluminum decay?

When I arrive in the country, the first snow is on the ground, and the soil is hard. The burial will have to wait till spring. The water pipe for the garden is frozen, so my mother's pressure cooker comes in handy, I fill it to the brim with snow and put it on the stove so that I can use the warm water to thaw out the frozen pipe. The snow melts, revealing a few brown autumn leaves that were lying in the grass when the snow began to fall. The hotter the snow broth becomes, the more quickly the leaves swirl around in the pot, the stronger the smell of decay.

In a cold, winterized kitchen with no running water, in a small house that can only be inhabited in the summer, my mother's pressure cooker has become a pot once again: I am cooking—a soup of black leaves.

JANUARY 2010

John

The telephone rings. Who is it? I'm not telling. I want to play you something. *Michelle, ma belle.* The telephone rings. Who is it? I'm not telling, I want to play you something. *Yesterday.* The telephone rings. Who is it? I'm not telling. But I want to play you something. This goes on for weeks. How do we know each other? I'm not telling. *A Hard Day's Night.* I'm going to hang up if you don't tell me your name. You can call me John. *Yellow Submarine.* Like John Lennon. But what's your real name? I'm not telling. "You are like a flower, so fair and fine and pure." The letter in our mailbox doesn't have a stamp. How do we know each other? Guess. *P.S. I Love You.* We talk about music. We talk about the cold world of adults. We talk about the nuclear threat. A letter arrives with the word "peace" repeated over and over to form the letters of my name. *You really got a hold on me.* A letter arrives with a text by Wolfgang Borchert: "You, the girl behind the counter, and the girl in the office. If they order you tomorrow to fill grenades and assemble scopes for sniper rifles, there's only one answer: Say no!" *Love, lo-o-ove, love.* I get used to these calls from John Lennon, I lay the receiver on the table and let the music play while I do my homework. *I want to hold your hand.* A letter arrives that lists all of the people who entered or exited the high-rise where I live on a given Wednesday between 3 and 5 p.m. 1 man in a light coat (exiting). 1 woman with a string shopping bag (entering). 2 children (exiting). 1 old woman with a dog (exiting), etc. The list is long. I don't appear on the list, and neither does my mother. I was at a friend's house that afternoon, my mother didn't enter or exit. Why do you sit there for hours? Why did you do that? *Love, lo-o-ove, love.* Do you even know what I look like? *Do you want to know a secret.* Do we know each other?

Ten years later, well into adulthood, I've already learned a trade, and I'm studying at the university, the wall has fallen. I request my Stasi file, which isn't very thick. One of the few pages contains my personal information with the comment: Pacifist. I'm surprised. I turn the page. "You, the girl behind the counter, and the girl in the office. If they order you tomorrow to fill grenades and assemble scopes for sniper rifles, there's only one answer: Say no!" I turn the page:

```
Peace, peace, peace,
Peace, peace, peace,
Peace, peace, peace.
Peace, peace, peace,            Peace, peace, peace,
Peace, peace, peace,        Peace, peace, peace, peace, peace
Peace, peace, peace,        Peace, peace,            peace, peace,
Peace, peace, peace,    Peace, peace, peace, peace, peace, peace
Peace, peace, peace,    Peace, peace, peace, peace, peace, peace,
Peace, peace, peace,        Peace, peace,
Peace, peace, peace.        Peace, peace, peace, peace, peace,
Peace, peace, peace,            Peace, peace, peace, peace,
Peace, peace, peace,                Peace, peace, peace.
```

etc.

I turn the page. And find: 1 man in a light coat (exiting). 1 woman with a string shopping bag (entering). 2 children (exiting). 1 old woman with a dog (exiting). This is probably the only case in Stasi history when the surveillance authority intercepted a letter from a high school boy who kept a high school girl's house under surveillance because he was in love with her. I have to think of the words spoken by Erich Mielke, the head of the Stasi: But I love all of you. *Love, lo-o-ove, love.* From my Stasi file, a part of my youth that I had almost forgotten looks back at me. One day, just when I least expected it, John finally revealed his identity after all. His real name was Sebastian, and he was a skinny, pale boy who had fallen in love with me when I played a mermaid in a pageant at summer camp.

JANUARY 2012

Homesick for Sadness

So what was I doing the night the wall fell?

I spent that evening with friends, just a few blocks from the spot where world history was being made, and then: I slept. I literally slept through that moment of world history, and while I was asleep, the pot wasn't just being stirred, it was being knocked over and smashed to bits. The next morning I learned: We didn't even need pots anymore.

In the society that I had been born into, the most radical critics of the government had outdone the government itself in hoping. So I had learned to hope—to live with the provisional status of things, to know better, and to wait. But what now? Now the people who had gotten it wrong weren't just being replaced, they were being written off completely. And those who had known better were suddenly left sitting in an empty theater. There was suddenly a lot of talk of *freedom*, but I couldn't make much of this word *freedom*, which floated freely in all sorts of sentences. *Freedom* to travel? (But will we be able to afford it?) Or *freedom* of opinion? (What if no one cares about my opinion?) *Freedom* to shop? (But what happens when we're finished shopping?) *Freedom* wasn't given freely, it came at a price, and the price was my entire life up to that point. The price was that everything that had been called the present until then was now called the past. Our everyday lives weren't everyday lives anymore, they were an adventure that we had survived, our customs were suddenly an attraction. In the course of just a few weeks, what had been self-evident ceased to be self-evident. A door that opens only once a century had opened, but now the century was also gone forever. From that moment on, my childhood belonged in a museum.

Recently, I opened the newspaper to find an obituary for my elementary school.

Yes, really. Former students had placed a memorial in the newspaper for the building where I had attended school for eight years of my childhood. *Today we quietly mourn the demolition of our school.* But these students, who are all adults now, didn't just use the unusually long obituary to express their grief, they also wrote about their everyday lives at and with the school, which was built in 1973–74 in the valley between the East Berlin high-rises in Leipziger Strasse and the Springer high-rise in West Berlin—it was a standard, boxy modern building that later served as a high school for about ten years after reunification before being abandoned, and then it stood empty for another ten years, gradually becoming overgrown with trees, bushes, and weeds. A silent place, maybe one square kilometer including the athletic field, right around the corner from the hustle and bustle of Checkpoint Charlie, an international tourist attraction for anyone who wants to know what the wall felt like. And just a fifteen-minute walk from Potsdamer Platz, with its glass palaces.

Where else could something like that be found in a Western capital, an abandoned lot right in the middle of the city, a barren piece of earth, a dead remnant of the everyday life of another era? Ground Zero in New York was transformed into a construction site as soon as the wreckage had been hauled away, and at the edge of the construction site a museum was built to commemorate those who had died in the World Trade Center attack. But no one had died in our school. There hadn't been a war or an act of terror, thank god. Once the authorities had abandoned our school, the site represented nothing more than a new society's impatience for an empty lot in a prime location.

When I go to see the rubble heap today, only a small piece of the rear stairwell is still intact. That was the stairwell that led to the science classrooms when I was a student there. At recess, the boys from my class would stand in the niche between this stairwell and the wall of the actual school building, forming a tight circle with their backs to everyone else, so that they could smoke in secret. When one of them became *my boyfriend*, that made me the first girl who got to stand there at recess and turn my back to everyone else.

What actually happens to the curvature of space-time when a wall collapses, when the ceiling crashes to the floor?

Places always disappear in two stages, this becomes clear to me for the first time when I notice something beside the large rubble heap, a droopy mountain of red rubber mats that used to cover the athletic field. The first stage: the place is emptied out, grown over, it collapses, but it's still there—and then the second: the place is wiped away, and something else moves in. Only after it has been wiped away, cleared off, disposed of, can the place that was once there give way to something else.

That derelict fermata in the midst of Berlin Mitte had at least been a sort of placeholder all that time for my memories of the school, although certainly it wasn't always a happy place, schools seldom are. A wilderness right in the center of the up-and-coming neighborhood of Mitte, this single square kilometer was also something like a bygone era that sticks in the throat of the new one until it can finally be spit out.

Only when the surface has been smoothed out, when all visible traces have been removed, do this forgotten place and the forgotten time contained within it proceed down their final path, becoming a purely mental state, if you will, from then on they will no longer exist anywhere except in the convolutions of my brain and the convolutions of certain other brains, each will find its final refuge in one memory or another.

Outside the school's main entrance, there was a plaza big enough for all of the students to assemble in a square formation for the flag ceremony. We also gathered there when the administration held a fire drill. And from April or May on we would play a game there according to our own strict rules, jumping over elastic bands that were tied together and stretched between two girls' legs. We used waistband elastic, and back then we called the game *Gummihopse*, today most Germans would probably say *Gummitwist*, in America they call it Chinese jump rope. For the first round, the bands would be at ankle height; for the second round at the knees; for the third round at the hips. The jumps that allowed you to move your two feet separately were always easier than those that required you to hop over one of the bands with both feet together. The school's front steps, which led from this plaza of games, flag-raisings, and fire drills to the main entrance, also served as the backdrop for our annual class photos, with the taller students arrayed on the steps behind the shorter ones, as in a choir.

A plaza that's just the right size for all of the students to assemble in a square formation for the flag ceremony (*Where's my blue pleated skirt? Where's my cap? Why isn't it staying on? Come here, I'll fasten it with a bobby pin! No, that hurts!*), a plaza like that is covered in slabs of cement, and when a plaza like that is covered in slabs of cement, then it's a good place for jumping over an elastic band stretched between two girls' legs. A flag-raising can be a routine, and so can a game that girls play when the weather is finally warm enough to wear knee socks.

There, on the spot where that plaza used to be, the students are all gone now, and the word *flag-raising* is a term that has served its purpose, a rubble word. There, on that spot that was left empty to make room for the students' orderly assemblies, pieces of concrete from the demolished building have now piled up, one on top of the other. This mountain of concrete has a special significance to me, because on one of those pieces I can see the small blue tiles that covered the girls' bathroom. Did I like that bathroom? Is it even possible to like a school bathroom? Don't I look forward to the future? To the apartments or offices with great natural light that will soon take the place of this former socialist school bathroom? To granite, stainless steel, oak, in place of the classroom bulletin boards bearing slogans like: *The Fire Started with a Spark!* To elevators with doors that softly close, in place of the open air where students responded to the command *For peace and socialism—be prepared!* with a snappy or weary *Always prepared!*

No, strangely enough it has nothing to do with the question of whether the past that is now being replaced was pleasant or unpleasant, good or evil, honest or dishonest. It was simply time, time that really did pass in this way that I knew, and that was preserved in those rooms. Time that was once the present, a shared present that included my own personal present. Time that entailed a particular concept of the future which I knew well, even if that future itself remained a very distant one. *The future isn't what it used to be*, Karl Valentin said it well. By now I know what became of the bright future that our school was preparing us for. The hard slog, what Brecht called the "struggles of the plain," in contrast to the "struggles of the mountain." That plain proved to be too wide. But what now? Now there's another future. Or do the present and the future now merge together forever? And when these ruins are cleared away once and for all, will the past be written off once and for all, too? Are we arriving, now and forever, in an era that claims validity for all time?

Now that the school basement, which was sometimes used as a vaccination clinic, and the cafeteria, which still served dishes like *blood sausage with sauerkraut*, and the auditorium, where our pictures from art class hung, have been reduced to rubble, I see that the two stages of disappearance mentioned above correspond to two stages of grief for me. As the building slowly decayed, I initially grieved for those specific places: the vaccination clinic, the cafeteria, the auditorium. Not for the rooms themselves, of course, but for those rooms as the setting for my everyday childhood experiences, a setting that was slowly rotting away—as if that everyday life, so far in the past, could also grow old and weak in retrospect.

But as this rubble is wiped away, I begin to experience a more fundamental sort of grief that transcends my own biography: grief for the disappearance of a place that was such a visible injury, for the disappearance of sick or disturbed things or spaces, which offer proof that the present can't *make its peace* with everything, an apt expression. In this second stage, the *cleansing* stage, I grieve for the disappearance of unfinished or broken things as such, of those things that had visibly refused until now to be incorporated into the whole, the disappearance of the dirt, if you will. In places where grass *just grows*, where trash piles up, human order is put into perspective. And considering that every one of us is mortal, it's never a bad thing to bear that perspective in mind.

Where the socialist architects wanted to keep the evil spirits out, there wasn't enough concrete, thank god, or at least it cracked. And they couldn't do everything at once. Spare parts were hard to come by. And besides: Who owned the *property of the people*, anyway? Who was responsible for it? When I was a child, everything I saw in this city was also a reminder that the present of that socialist experiment was not so far removed from the presence of war. The unfinished present and the vision of a bright future, the destroyed past and the construction sites where the new world was being built, still existed side by side, you could see them any time. *Resurrected from the ruins, faces toward the future turned,* that was the first line of the East German national anthem, and you couldn't have one without the other, the future without the ruins. And after all, children first begin to learn from the things that are *there,* they learn by seeing what's *there*, what exists side by side in that moment. Stories only come later, individual experiences. For children, the ruins of bygone eras that ended before they were born aren't initially places of mourning, any more than hospitals are places of mourning for children who have never seen anyone close to them suffer there, or cemeteries, when they have never buried a friend, a grandmother, a grandfather, a father or mother. Ruins aren't even places of fear for children, because they lack the experience that would inspire that fear. My own love of dirt, let's just call it that, of unfinished things and ruins, was an unburdened love when I was a child, and what I learned, I learned thanks to the simple presence of such damaged places and spaces, their mere existence, the fact that I shared the days of my life with them.

Ruins were an everyday sight in my childhood, those very ruins that had cost me nothing, that belonged to the reality into which I had been born. Didn't I have my first rendezvous with the high school boyfriend I mentioned earlier in the ruins of the Deutscher Dom, between weeds and jagged blocks of stone? Hadn't I climbed the strong branches of a birch tree, which reached all the way up to the second floor, to enter the ruins of the New Museum, to enter the one half of a hallway that still remained intact, to see the statues that no one else knew were there? Those statues that were conceived as torsos from the start, but had suffered additional injuries in a war in which they had no stake? Hadn't my father always told the same story as we drove past Alexanderplatz in our Trabant, pointing to the construction fence across from Berlin's Town Hall and recalling the mummified bodies from the Biedermeier era that he had seen there as a student, in the catacombs that had survived the war beneath St. Nicholas's Church, bodies that probably still lay there under the rubble of that bombed-out quarter? I knew the bullet holes that pocked the bases of Humboldt University, of the State Library, and of all the other major buildings in Mitte, I always knew what it looks like when a tree grows out of a rain gutter, knew what it's like to look out a window onto an air-raid shelter, and knew the washed-out colors on a brick wall that remains when the rest of the house has been destroyed, showing where the bathroom, the kitchen, the pantry used to be. Steel girders. Charred beams. Walls with nothing behind them. Rooms where the rain falls on dead pigeons because there isn't a roof overhead. Fire walls that make pretty silhouettes at sunset. Cordoned-off areas. Empty spaces and dead-ends right in the center of Berlin Mitte.

As a child I loved the ruins. They were secret places, unoccupied places where the weeds grew up to your knees, and no adults ever followed us there. Sometimes they were also dangerous places, places with pretty views, places where we could make discoveries that were ours alone. Quiet places where nothing happened, nothing but the clouds passing overhead. Places where you could look up through several floors and burned-out windows to see the sky. Places where shepherd's purse grew, with heart-shaped pods that you could eat. Places that formed a landscape in the middle of the city. Only later did I understand that what seemed so familiar to my childhood eyes was actually another era, a destroyed era that sticks in the throat of the new one until it can finally be spit out. But there was one difference: It didn't cost anything for the ruins to stand there back then. Time wasn't running, time was standing still. No one talked about money. The private ownership of land had been abolished. Real estate lived up to its legal name, "immovable property"—it was simply there, unmoving.

It was probably during that time that I learned to live with unfinished things, and with the knowledge that houses built for eternity aren't really eternal. Only as an adult did I learn that when Hitler planned the major building projects for his *Thousand-Year Reich*, he intended them to be magnificent ruins even after those thousand years had come to an end. So the destroyed city of Berlin offered many opportunities to learn which parts of a dome or a department store survive, to learn that it's possible to live quite comfortably in the bottom two floors of an apartment building even when the top two floors have been bombed to rubble. And that's the sort of knowledge that you never forget. Even today, without thinking too much about it, I automatically transform all shopping malls into the ruins of shopping malls, I see clouds of dust rising up in luxury boutiques, I imagine the glass facades of office buildings shattering and crashing to the ground, revealing the naked offices behind them where no one is working anymore. I know very well what it would be like if all of the rubber trees in the living rooms and all of the geraniums on the balconies dried up because no one was there to water them, or because the people who *were* there had more urgent tasks to attend to than watering their plants. I see fountains full of wreckage, I see streets that are no longer passable, and I wonder which pieces of furniture in my apartment might still have a piece of floor left to stand on when the rest of the apartment is no longer there. Similarly, I've always known how the people sitting across from me on the subway— children, teenagers, adults in the prime of life—will look when they're 80 years old, I've had no choice but to transform those people into their own ruins, too, into sick, wise, barren, or overripe ruins of faces and bodies, I've known what kind of decay awaits them, and I've seen it again and again in different forms. This compulsion for transformation is still with me today, as if the decay of everything in existence were simply the other half of the world, without which nothing could be imagined.

And at the same time, I myself was living right in the middle of a construction site that could only be there because nothing, or almost nothing, remained from before—but I didn't even understand what I was experiencing. And that's probably always the case: It takes us an entire lifetime to unravel the mysteries of our own lives. Layer upon layer of knowledge accumulates upon the past, revealing it anew each time as a past that we certainly lived through, but couldn't even begin to understand.

I start with my life as a schoolgirl, I grow, and the houses around our house grow, too. My own conscious life begins at the same time as the socialist life of Leipziger Strasse, which today leads to Potsdamer Platz, though back then it came to an end at the wall. Today I know that a hundred years ago, Leipziger Strasse was a narrow, popular, and very lively commercial thoroughfare, with tobacconists, a horse-drawn tram, houses with ornate sandstone facades, and women in pretty hats. Jewish textile factories did business in that neighborhood until the early 1930s. But by the time I was a child, all of that was gone, and I didn't even know that anything was missing—or anyone. Today I also know that the high-rises, including the one I lived in, were very consciously conceived as propaganda instruments, a counterpart to the Springer high-rise in the West, but when I was a child I was simply thrilled when we could look down on New Year's Eve from the terrace above the 23rd floor and see the many flashes of light below. In school, we read the time for our socialist recess from a glowing clock in the western part of the city that we could see on the other side of the wall. The fact that the building that displayed the clock also displayed the letters *BZ*—an advertisement for a newspaper that we didn't know—was of no interest to us. On our Sunday strolls, my parents took me down to the end of Leipziger Strasse, to the neighborhood that abutted the wall, it was as quiet as a village there, with smooth asphalt from before the war where I could roller-skate, the bus line ended there, and there was no through traffic. That was where the earth came to an end. There is nothing better for a child than to grow up at the ends of the earth.

When I was a child, one half of the city seemed like a whole to me. Even today, although I understand that the city is finally functioning again as intended, by growth and by design, my feelings disagree. For instance, I can drive along Chaussee Strasse a hundred times, from the East Berlin neighborhood of Mitte to the West Berlin neighborhood of Wedding—by now it's a perfectly normal street again—but every single time, a hundred times, I drive through a border crossing. The two parts have grown back together, but for me it isn't a question of growing back together, instead it's a completely arbitrary addition, since when I was a child I never experienced the two halves of Berlin as *one* city. I see how the standard operations of a capitalist metropolis are moving back into the buildings on the side that I knew well, buildings that they already occupied fifty years earlier, and I understand now that these buildings always knew more than they could tell me. *Haus der Schweiz*—I had never understood what that building with a ground-floor grocery store along the socialist boulevard Unter den Linden had to do with Switzerland. But now the building belongs to the banks and insurance companies again, as it did when it was built. And yet—what I didn't learn back then, with the feelings of a child, I can never make up for now, with the feelings of an adult. For someone like my old neighbor—who always bought his rolls at the bakery across the street before the war, until suddenly, from one day to the next, that side of the street was in the West—just the opposite must have been the case. When he had the feelings of a child, he encountered Berlin as *one* city; for him, I imagine, the wall must have been a subtraction that lasted twenty-eight years.

When I was a child, I didn't differentiate between the ruins that the Second World War had left behind and the empty lots and city-planning absurdities that resulted from the construction of the wall. The buildings still painted with the words "Dairy" or "Coal Merchant" in the gothic script of the Nazi era, even though no dairy or coal shop had been there for years, were an everyday sight when I was a child growing up in the seventies, just like the subway station entrances that had been closed off ever since the wall was built. The wind blew old paper and dry leaves to the bottom of those stairs, which no one went down for thirty years; as children in the East, we could sometimes hear the sounds of the West Berlin subways through the ventilation grates as they passed underneath the East without stopping, we knew the warm air that drifted up to us from those inaccessible air shafts, but we learned that just as the municipal dairies and coal shops could disappear forever, there were also paths beneath our feet that were not meant for us, airplanes overhead in which we would never fly, we heard the construction workers on the scaffolding in West Berlin hammering and drilling, and we knew that an entire world that seemed so close could remain inaccessible nonetheless.

But at the same time we learned—if you look at it from another perspective—that alongside the world we knew, right next to it in fact, there was a whole other world. We learned—without learning, just by being in this city and living this life—that the things within reach weren't all that there was. That there were other worlds concealed beneath the earth we walked on, and in the sky where clouds floated across both sides of the city, East and West, undisturbed. When I was a child, an empty space didn't strike me as evidence of a lack, it was a space that adults had either abandoned or forbidden, and so now, at least in my imagination, it belonged entirely to me.

I often stood by the curtains in my grandmother's living room, looking at the large building that could be seen on the other side of the wall, *over there*. It may have been a school or a barracks. In the morning, the whole building was bathed in sunlight. I liked it, and I wondered what kind of people lived or worked there. The wall, which separated me from the part of the city where that building stood, and the barricades in front of the wall, and the strip of sand where those barricades stood, which was probably mined, and the border guard patrolling right below me, were significantly less interesting to me. While my grandmother was complaining that a dust rag that she'd hung out to dry on the balcony railing had blown into the border strip and been lost forever, I would keep my eye on that building. In the evening, the lights in the windows stayed on late, the same fluorescent light in every window, so they probably weren't apartments after all. An empty space is a space for questions, not for answers. And what we don't know is infinite.

My aunt, who sent me the best care packages from West Berlin, lived on Sickingen Strasse. The address was on the packing paper. Sickingen Strasse. *The Trumpeter of Sickingen*, I thought throughout my childhood, but actually the story is called *The Trumpeter of Säckingen*. And the *Trumpeter of Säckingen*, as I understood even then, certainly couldn't be the same trumpeter I thought of when I sang the *Song of the Little Trumpeter*: "Of a-a-all our comrades, there was none so kind and good, as our little trumpeter, with his merry Red Guard blood, his merry Red Guard blood." But when you're a child, it doesn't surprise you if the son of a Baroque burgher from Säckingen sings Erich Weinert's communist trumpeter's song in the inaccessible

Sickingen Strasse in West Berlin. That song always moved me to tears, and so as a child I believed that Sickingen Strasse must be a beautiful street, a beautiful street in the inaccessible West, where the scents of *Ariel* detergent and *Jacobs Krönung* coffee would drift in the air, while the little trumpeter was dying his melodious hero's death.

After the wall fell I eventually went to visit my aunt, and it turned out, inevitably enough, that Sickingen Strasse wasn't beautiful and fragrant at all, but loud and dirty, and my aunt's apartment was in a modest postwar building from the 1950s—a living room, a bedroom, a kitchen, a bathroom—a dark space with low ceilings, built-in shelving, ornamental cups and saucers, a corner sofa. Peeking out from between the curtains, I saw the *Employment Office* sign on the building across the street, and saw the many sad-looking men standing in front of it, apparently waiting for the office to finally open. Even with the windows closed, I could hear the sound of the nearby expressway from inside my aunt's quiet living room. So the liberated West didn't look, didn't smell, didn't sound at all like the West had back when it was blossoming in my young mind.

From the other side, though, the unknown was probably just as great a mystery, like a vacuum that quickly fills up with stories. *How gray it was in East Berlin*, said the visitors from the West who dared to set foot in the eastern part of the city. Only now can I imagine what an adventure it must have been back then, stepping into that forbidden zone after paying the price of admission by exchanging twenty-five West German marks for East German currency. Later, when I was a teenager living close to the border crossing at Friedrich Strasse, Westerners would sometimes give me the leftover twenty-mark bills that they hadn't managed to spend in the East. Those Westerners sometimes looked a bit embarrassed that they were treating me like a beggar, they looked like they didn't understand at all how the East actually worked, and they looked happy that they could return to the place they understood.

In reality, though, East Berlin probably wasn't so much grayer than the West after all, at least that's my impression now that I know the West, the only things missing in the East were the advertising posters and neon signs decorating the pockmarked walls or concealing the bombed-out lots. True, there was plaster crumbling from the walls of the buildings in Prenzlauer Berg, and there were some balconies that could no longer be used because they'd fallen into disrepair. True, the front doors of the apartment buildings weren't locked, because private property wasn't important, so sometimes a drunk would piss in the entryway. Fair enough.

But what I remember most of all, gray or not, was an almost small-town sense of calm, as a child it gave me a strong impression that I was at home—in a world that was closed off, and thus completely and utterly safe. Seen from the outside, our everyday life under socialism might have seemed exotic, but we weren't a wonder or a horror to ourselves, we were the everyday world, and in that everyday world we were among ourselves. The only things that connected us as children to the so-called big wide world outside were the care packages from the West (but not everyone got those) and *international solidarity*, the worldwide struggle for the release of Luis Corvalán or Angela Davis, for example, and as children we translated those grand efforts into very manageable forms, like bake sales or recycling drives, donating all of the proceeds to the cause. My parents' furniture was in the Biedermeier style, and our money was light like play money. Political immaturity wasn't a burden, as long as you were actually a child. As a child, you love what you know. Not the things that adults enjoy. Or strangers. Just the things that you know. You are happy to know anything at all. And this happiness takes root and transforms itself into the feeling of being at home. And so, yes, I loved that ugly, supposedly gray East Berlin, forgotten by the whole world but familiar to me, which doesn't exist anymore, at least not in the part where I lived as a child.

When my son and I are in the countryside in the summer, we sometimes roam around, crawl through the gaps in crooked fences to explore abandoned sites, the former company holiday camps where workers spent their summer vacations with their families, we open the doors of the empty bungalows—they aren't even locked—and look quietly at the carefully folded wool blankets at the foot of each bunk bed, at the curtains that someone dutifully closed before departing long, long ago, at the *Mitropa* cups that someone returned to the kitchen shelf twenty-five years ago after washing them. I look with him—while neither of us says a word—at all of those things that have remained unchanged, as if under a spell, since the last socialist vacationers spent their annual vacation here, right before their companies were *liquidated* in the early nineties, and an absence that was only supposed to last two days became an absence that lasts forever.

Now the *milk break* will last forever in the museum of my memory, I drink vanilla milk out of a small, pyramid-shaped container, the opening slowly gets softer as I drink, I think of the mechanical pencils that we unscrewed to make blowguns for spitballs, think of the notes we wrote and passed to each other, of the laughing fits that my best friend and I had in the last row; I remember how we rocked back and forth in our chairs or played with pins and buttons and erasers, hidden from view behind an open pencil case, and I remember clearly the first morning when I had to come to class with glasses perched on my nose, everyone said that I looked just like Lilo Herrmann now, the antifascist resistance fighter whose picture was in our textbook, who seemed dreadfully ugly to all of us back then just because she wore horn-rimmed glasses; but my most vivid memory is of the day when I stood up in the middle of class, walked across the room, and gave the boy who always teased me a slap across the face to make an impression—and he slapped me back: a form of revenge so unchivalrous that it shocked me. The red mark on my cheek was still visible at recess. Just a few days later, it seemed perfectly natural when that same boy became *my boyfriend*.

Now the place where all of that happened is flat, like a closed book, and as I stand beside it, I know: That's where I learned to read. The desert isn't the opposite of a mountain, it's just a spread-out mountain, the mountain climber Reinhold Messner once said. My very normal school days—which ultimately weren't very different from thousands of other school days— only became something noteworthy when the place where they played out was torn down, when the society that shaped that place disappeared. But everything that can't be seen there anymore lives in my head now instead, more vivid than ever. Only for a while, of course, since memories are engraved in mortal flesh, and the older I grow, the more blurred and confused those memories will become, until ultimately they are wiped away along with me, once and for all, so that in the very same place where I used to walk around in this world with my memories of all sorts of things, someone else can walk around with memories of something else.

JUNE 2013

Hope

When my great-grandfather was young, he hoped that by changing his name from Gmora to Braun, he could make his life go more smoothly.

When my great-grandmother was a widow, she didn't allow her late husband's brother into her home when he unexpectedly arrived from somewhere near Kishinev. She was a friendly person. The only explanation I can think of for her unfriendliness is hope: that her children would have an easier time under Hitler without their Jewish relatives.

When my grandmother was a young woman, she hoped to return home from a Soviet prison camp to her three children.

When my grandmother was deported to the prison camp, my great-grandmother hoped her daughter would come home.

When my mother was a small child, she perched on my great-grandmother's lap and hoped the bombs would fall on other houses.

When the family had to leave East Prussia, my great-grandmother hoped she would survive the journey with her three small grandchildren.

When my mother was stuck on a crowded platform outside the departing train, while my great-grandmother was already sitting inside the train with my uncle and aunt, my great-grandmother hoped the Red Army soldier would manage to pass the small girl over the heads of all the waiting people and through the window of the train before it departed.

When my grandmother returned from the prison camp, she hoped she would remember the names of her three children.

When my mother was a child, she hoped no one would notice that she had broken the rules and jumped over the creek—and fallen in. But when she undressed that evening, her underwear was green with algae.

When my mother was a young girl, she hoped Sundays would pass more quickly.

When my mother was pregnant for the second time, she hoped that she would have the child this time, and that it would be healthy.

When my mother was a mother, she hoped nothing would happen to me.

When I was a small child and my mother was away on a trip, I hoped my father would let me wear my blue pleated skirt on an ordinary weekday, even though it was supposed to be reserved for the flag ceremony. My father didn't know much about those things.

When my grandmother's birthday rolled around, she hoped she'd be able to finish baking the bee sting cake in time for her party.

When I was a child, I once hid in the wooden chest and hoped someone would notice I was missing.

When my grandmother traveled with us, she always hoped her suitcase could be closed.

When my great-grandmother was a very old woman, she hoped her daughter, who lived with her, wouldn't be so impatient with her.

After my mother had gotten divorced for the second time, my grandmother hoped some nice man would give this difficult woman another chance.

After my mother had gotten divorced for the second time, she hoped to find another man who wouldn't cheat on her.

When I was a young woman, I hoped my mother wouldn't cry the day I moved out.

When my mother's third husband was on his deathbed, I hoped he wouldn't die.

After he died, I hoped my mother wouldn't kill herself.

When I had my child, my mother hoped the birth would be easier for me than my birth had been for her.

When I became a mother, I hoped things would always go well for my child.

When my son was older, my mother hoped she would live long enough to see him start school.

When my grandmother waved goodbye to me, I hoped it was just an ordinary goodbye, like all of the ones in the previous years.

On Christmas, I hoped our son wouldn't notice that my father was Santa Claus.

When I heard that my mother had had a stroke and fallen into a coma, I hoped the doctors were wrong, that she had only fainted.

When I sat next to my mother's bed as she was dying, I hoped that this day hadn't really come yet, that it was still two days ago.

After my mother died, I went to Switzerland for work. While everyone was talking behind me, I sat alone on a terrace with a view of the mountains. I hoped that up there I was close enough to my mother to see her.

Hope was always a sort of glue that held my family together. Some of my family's hopes were fulfilled, others were not.

2014

Time

Ladies and Gentlemen,

A few days ago, I watched as gardeners who were preparing to rake leaves in a park hung their plastic bags of breakfast rolls from the bushes.

When I watch concerts on TV, I often wish that the camera didn't always show the oboist at the moment when the oboe enters, but instead showed someone like the 4th french horn player, waiting his turn to play again.

In the translation of the *Iliad*, there's a nice passage where Achilles says: "Cattle and fat sheep can all be had for the raiding, / tripods all for the trading, and tawny-headed stallions. / But a man's life breath cannot come back again— / no raiders in force, no trading brings it back, / once it slips through a man's clenched teeth."*

Once, when I was searching for documents related to my family in the archive of this academy, I was surprised to see my own name in the list of search results, and I saw that a letter I had written to one of my teachers years ago was already in the archive. But the older me could only read what the younger me had written once I had proven that I was still the same person. My ID card did the trick. Then I read the letter, but I didn't recognize myself anymore.

Time has the power to separate us, not only from others, but also from ourselves—a fact that's hard to grasp. We know that time also separates us from circumstances that might have turned

---

* Homer, *The Iliad*, trans. Robert Fagles (New York: Penguin, 1991), 265.

us into very different people. We know it, but we don't understand it. In Germany there's even a special expression for it: *the grace of late birth.* Even so, we don't really understand it. Time also separates us from what's coming. Down on the ground, where the bushes' roots are concealed under the earth, the men are raking up the leaves, while their breakfast, their future, is dangling up above. *What will things be like in a year?* I asked my mother once. And my mother said: *We can just be happy that we don't know.*

We know only one thing: That behind everything we can see, hear, and touch, another reality is concealed—a reality that we can't see and can't hear and can't touch, a reality made of time. We know that transformations lie before us, we know that transformations lie behind us, and we know, according to scientific findings, that the present belongs to us for precisely 3 seconds before it plunges down the throat of the past. That means that every 3 seconds, we produce ourselves again as strangers.

What should I say, then, when I'm asked to say who I am?

Should I say that I'm someone whose childhood can now only be seen in a museum, or in black-and-white photographs? Rows of crumbling houses, the *Fernsehturm,* happy Pioneers, a workers' brigade party with dancing, and so on?

Or: I'm someone whose father's parents fled *from* Germany at the beginning of the war, and whose mother's family fled *to* Germany at the end of the war?

Should I say: In the forest where I played in the summer, grass grew over the trenches.

Or are the important things something else entirely? For example:

Once I opened a cupboard because I heard a noise, and I found a rat sitting inside, startled at the sight of me.

Or:

I can still picture the hand of a friend of mine who died of cancer.

Or:

I find it absurd to buy shoes that cost 400 euros.

It's really not so easy to find sentences that explain who you are. But maybe it's not so important, either. Maybe it's more important that beyond the borders of our own skin, beyond the borders of language, and beyond the various individual branches of the arts, we are engaged in a collective attempt to make something visible, audible, or perhaps indeed legible: the forgetting that lies behind us all, the unknown that contains us all, and the inconspicuous places where our own present takes shape. Our reflections on the ways that we see, hear, and read, and our interest in the perceptions of others, are, I hope, a foreshadowing of a world in which difference is a topic of discussion, but not a reason to kill anyone.

I thank you for transforming me into a member of this academy.

NOVEMBER 2015

LITERATURE AND MUSIC

Literary Role Models

From the moment I learned to read by myself, I have been reading. I read at home in the morning before school, I read in secret under the bench at school, I read on the toilet, I read as I walked down the street, I read while I was waiting, I read on the bus. My mother could ask me whatever she wanted, I just said *Yes* without listening, I was reading. From the moment I learned to read, and for many years thereafter, I read all of the folk and fairy tales I could find: German and Persian, Slovakian and Native American, Russian and French, the Grimms' and Hauff's and Andersen's and the *Thousand and One Nights*.

Cinderella's sister has to cut off her toes to fit into her sister's slipper.

The roc, that giant bird, catches me and carries me to an island where there are diamonds as big as fists.

The twelve months sit around a fire examining everyone who passes by.

The princess falls down a well and arrives in heaven.

A wolf is stuffed with stones while still alive.

The tales were full of transformations, full of dreams in which the essence of life unfolds, animated by the freedom that magic grants, but also caught under the spell of black magic. Children turn into stones, frogs into princes, princesses have to serve the servants at night. In these tales, the day bears traces of the nocturnal, the half-conscious, and there is always a second time alongside the time of reality, a second aspect to every place behind its outward appearance. Dwarf Nose serves a sorceress for a single day, but when he returns home, seven years have gone by. Wishes are fulfilled, but they are also fragile, genies build a splendid palace overnight, but when the tale's hero grows too bold, the palace dissolves into thin air. Alongside wishes there are curses, the wicked are cursed, but so are the just, and above all, places are cursed, places that await their redemption, that wait to be seen from the right angle, for their mysteries to be solved.

Everything that is human can be found in these tales, in all of its intensity and all of its harshness: No greater shame can be imagined than that of King Thrushbeard's bride at the moment when, in front of the entire court, the earthenware pot that she has hidden beneath her skirt shatters—the pot in which she intended to smuggle food home from the banquet to her impoverished life—and the food pours out. But alongside everything that is human in these tales, there is also the magical; and it is just as concrete, just as natural, just as real. The transformations in these tales expanded my reality like a drug. When Hans Fallada described Anna Barbara's descent into Hell—or rather into the domain of Hans Geiz—through a hole in a snow-covered stubble field, it seemed just as plausible to me as the transformation of the archivist Lindhorst into a vulture later would in E.T.A. Hoffmann's story; Lindhorst rises into the air at dusk, his coattails billowing about him. So I learned to read secret signs just as I was learning to read. I learned to let the stories behind the letters wash over me, as if I were swimming. To stop thinking, and to see only with my mind.

At the time, I assumed that these tales were supposed to end happily, so I approached them with that expectation, always prepared to keep searching for the Isles of the Blessed. And so as a teenager I arrived at the Rosenhaus in Adelbert Stifter's *Indian Summer*, where life is arranged in the service of beauty, where nature is recorded and ordered and organized according to new categories, the narrator has an inheritance that provides him with an income for life, and he roams through the mountains collecting botanical samples in his vasculum, learns to arrange statues in the proper light, he studies the trades of men with equanimity and kindness, engages in philosophical conversations, contemplates cameos and paintings, and everything that he does is filled with meaning and order—and free from the constraints to which people are otherwise subjected in their earthly existence. The Rosenhaus is the vision of an elite existence in freedom, a secure existence within an orderly world, but that order is not imposed from without, it is self-created. But even here, the narrator's freedom is not only spatial, it is also temporal. It is the narrator's good fortune to be able to choose his own tasks, and to allow for each of these tasks as much time as he deems necessary. From the very first page, the book puts the reader at ease, the same sort of ease that the narrator enjoys thanks to the circumstances of his life. Perhaps it was this sense of ease—or the nearly autistic organization of the world in this book—that made it seem to me like a place where my own thoughts could find refuge, an inward escape, a utopia, leading away from a system that sought to explain all things in worldly terms, and into a microscopic infinity.

Then, when I read Hermann Hesse's *Steppenwolf*—right around the usual age, I must have been about 15—this refuge took on a new meaning for me, one tied to the dark omen of suicide. Like a child who builds a tower and then, having finished it, joyfully knocks it down again, I began to be drawn to thought experiments that ended in collapse. One story I read then made a particularly profound impression on me: a devil shows two children how easy it is to make men out of clay, he lets the little clay men run around and work for a while for his own amusement—and then he takes a stone and drops it on them. He demonstrates to the children what different paths a life can take, and how every fork in the road, every decision point in life, produces new, but also very circumscribed possibilities and impossibilities for the remainder of that life.

This unforeseeable fate, the incomprehensible, the inexplicable, the destructive principle that human thought is powerless to avert, began to exert a hold on me; the castle with the hedge of thorns, where a kiss can still bring deliverance, was transformed into Franz Kafka's castle, the prince into the land surveyor who wallows with his sweetheart in the dim light of puddles of beer, and the petrified figures now spoke in Kafka's words: "If nobody comes, then nobody comes."*

The uncanny returned, but this time it remained, and the stories ended in dissonance. What was lost, stayed lost. What was transformed, stayed transformed. In one of the *Metamorphoses*, the story of Cyane, Ovid writes: "You might have seen / Her limbs softening, her bones becoming pliant, / Her nails losing stiffness. The slenderest parts / Melted away first: her dark blue hair, her fingers, / Her legs and her feet. It is a brief passage / From willowy limbs to chilly water. / Next her shoulders, back, and breasts / Vanish into rivulets, and in her veins / Clear water flows instead of blood, / And nothing is left that you could grasp."†

When the Grimms' tales make their way onto my reading list again, I don't even recognize them: The stories themselves seem to be transformed, because this time I'm reading the complete edition, which I had been spared as a child, so now I read: "'That was ill done, Hans, you should have cast friendly eyes on her.' 'Never mind, will do better.' Hans went into the stable, cut out all the calves' and sheep's eyes, and threw them in Gretel's face. Then Gretel became angry, tore herself loose and ran away, and was no longer the bride of Hans."‡

* Franz Kafka, "Excursion into the Mountains" in *The Complete Stories*, trans. Willa Muir and Edwin Muir (New York: Schocken, 1988), 383.
† Ovid, *Metamorphoses*, trans. Stanley Lombardo (Indianapolis: Hackett, 2010), 136.
‡ Jacob Grimm and Wilhelm Grimm, *The Complete Grimm's Fairy Tales*, trans. James Stern and Margaret Hunt (New York: Pantheon Books, 1972), 168.

Suddenly an icy humor prevails, a cold wind that blows from these archaic tales into the 20th century, where it cuts me to the bone as *The Lamentation of Dr. Faustus*. Now the devil is sitting in a plaid jacket on the horsehair sofa and laughing, like "churlish dross, a bawd," entertaining himself by occasionally changing from one form into another while negotiating the purchase of a soul.* Then, at the very end, when time has run out and Adrian Leverkühn is preparing to descend into Hell, he turns to his friends one last time: "Kindly beloved brethren and sisters."† Thus begins this speech of a condemned soul, an unrivaled, heart-rending farewell speech. But it is punctuated by the departure of a number of the invited guests who have grown weary of Leverkühn's madness and who begin first to cough quietly, then to murmur, then to stand, and finally to slip out, shaking their heads—they start their cars and drive back into the world. As a reader, I cry for the condemned man, but at the same time the cold, irreverent attitude of so many participants, who abscond in the face of Leverkühn's descent into Hell, moves me to despairing laughter. This has often been my experience with Thomas Mann, I have had to—*had to*—laugh, a laughter equal in measure to the horror. Djuna Barnes knows this sort of horror, too: "suddenly he had a notion that he was doing something that wasn't laughing at all, but something much worse, though he kept saying to himself, 'I am laughing, really laughing, nothing else whatsoever!'" When a girl is missing her legs, Barnes says that "the other half of her [is] still in God's bag of tricks!"‡

This uncanny hybrid of the speakable and the unspeakable, which passes for humor, was already familiar to me from the

---

* Thomas Mann, *Doctor Faustus*, trans. John E. Woods (New York: Knopf, 1997), 244.
† Ibid., 524.
‡ Djuna Barnes, *Nightwood* (New York: New Directions, 2006), 22, 29.

days of my childhood when I listened to Karl Valentin's records over and over as I played. The bookbinder Wanninger, who endlessly telephones to tell a customer that an order is ready, being transferred again and again from one person to the next but never actually reaching the responsible party, never managing to make his delivery. The man who lives in an apartment in the rear courtyard of a building, who inherits a mahogany bedroom suite from an unknown uncle in America and throws his own bedroom furniture out the window in eager anticipation of the arrival of his inheritance. When the bedroom suite arrives, it turns out that his uncle was a dwarf, the bed is a dwarf bed, the wardrobe a dwarf wardrobe, and no matter how he twists and turns, the heir can't fit into the bed, and his own shabby furniture lies smashed to bits in the courtyard below.

I encounter such lost souls again as I read the *Spoon River Anthology*, in which Edgar Lee Masters gives the dead residents of a small town ten or twenty lines each to describe the lives they have led. Alcoholics, secret affairs, crooked business dealings, old maids, lunatics, as well as some people who didn't drink, didn't make crooked deals, who just married this or that neighbor, didn't lose their minds—but all of them have died, each one a different death. All of that in ten or twenty lines.

This taciturnity—the few words actually spoken while so much remains unsaid—may be what ultimately inspired me to use language above all to give shape to the gaps between the words, those mute spaces, to give rhythm to the silence between the words. The pauses are part of the text, they may be the finest part, as I realized at some point, more by feeling than by understanding.

That had to do with music. As a young girl I sang in the church choir, I heard the biblical language again and again in the precision of Bach's recitatives:

"Jesus went with His disciples over the brook Cedron ..."

"... to be assessed with his betrothed Mary, who was pregnant."

"Let us not divide it, but cast lots upon it, whose it shall be."

I have never forgotten those phrases, even today they are with me in the melody of Bach's language, they have stayed with me because they are music. Now and then a feeling breaks through in the middle of the recitative, and the biblical text is stretched beyond its limits, as it is after Peter has denied Jesus: "he went out and wept bitterly."* There is no way to hold those tears in check. But the truly audacious passages are the transitions to the arias, a perfectly natural gesture by Baroque standards, in which someone suddenly begins to sing, someone who may not have even appeared yet as a character, but who might be said to speak for the soul of the singer himself. What agility of the spirit resides in this montage technique: This embedding of feeling in the dry stone of documentary is practically surreal. "Open your fiery abyss, O Hell, / crush, destroy, devour, shatter / with sudden rage / the false-hearted traitor, the murderous blood!"† These words are at once illuminating and devastating.

I had similar experiences when reading Guy de Maupassant, in whose stories real, thoroughly mundane events form the background against which otherworldly moments blaze up— for instance, I remember a tress of long, strawberry-blonde hair that flies through the room at the end of one of his stories; someone takes this strawberry-blonde tuft out of a cabinet and flings it across the room. Those are images that I absorbed through the language, but language was only the instrument that transferred them from one head to another, what arrived in my head and remained there was the image, the force of feeling, the shock. Some books haven't left any concrete turns of

* Johann Sebastian Bach, *St John Passion,* BWV 245, trans. Neil Jenkins, Thomas Alexander Lacey, and John Troutbeck (London: Novello, 1999), 50.
† Melvin P. Unger, *J. S. Bach's Major Works for Voices and Instruments: A Listener's Guide* (Lanham, MD: Scarecrow Press, 2005), 80, 85.

phrase in my memory, I may have even forgotten the authors, but they have taken hold of me, they live on to this day in my feelings, in my eyes, in my ears. I hear how admirably Madame Chauchat slams her door each morning, I hear the "fall of a little spoon at daybreak" with my ears, as if I had heard those sounds myself, my memories of those things are no different from my memories of real events in the past, those noises have filtered into my reading as the noises of reality filter into a light sleep, and they gave rise to dreams. I hear: "and at that moment I got heart failure for the rest of my life."*

DECEMBER 1999

---

* Barnes, *Nightwood*, 27.

Suction and Suggestion

When I open the door to my room, the air flows in from both sides, from the window and from the door, it seems as if the air from outside is just as eager to get in as the air from inside is to get out. Then one of the two—the window or the door—blows shut, the room is filled with fresher air, and everything is calm again.

Occasionally someone else enters the room while I'm sitting at my desk and the breeze whirls the papers on my desk into disarray, so I lunge for the window to close it and restore order, but in the process my elbow knocks my coffee cup—my favorite mug—off of the desk, and just at that moment, behind the guest, the door slams shut with a bang. The mug lies smashed to pieces on the floor, and everything is calm again.

Physically speaking, a draft like this is a form of suction, a process that restores equilibrium. Temperatures or objects in space tend toward equilibrium, and this tendency is so powerful that some things get dragged down, or pulled up, or away, things that actually belonged together and wanted to stay together. This tendency—of the many to overrun the few, of heat to cool, of emptiness to fill up—has its consequences. Houses are spun around, villages sink into the depths, people and animals drown, a child nurses its mother dry. "What hidden power ... / Draws me from these beloved horrors / Against my will, and conducts me / To the hateful light?" asks Orpheus, after he has turned to look at Eurydice and been sent back to the surface of the earth as punishment, against his will.* The great misfortune of disempowerment, the great fortune of disempowerment.

---

* Claudio Monteverdi, *Orfeo: A Tale in Music*, trans. Gilbert Blin (Vancouver, BC: EMV Masterworks Series, 2017), 17.

The end of the vortex is always unforeseeable. In Europe, the water in a bathtub spins counterclockwise as it runs down the drain, in Australia it spins clockwise. If only we could know what it looks like where those two spirals meet, spinning toward each other through the earth, at what point those two tubs of dirty bathwater reach a state of calm.

And if only we could know what wonderful depths Heinrich Heine's fisherman reaches after he sinks, and how he has been doing ever since. What equilibrium did he hope to attain by allowing himself to be sucked down into the depths? And does he enjoy the paradisiacal calm there that our ancestors enjoyed until they were expelled and banished? Banishment exerts a pull, a suction, and the less we know about what lies behind the wall, the more space remains for wishful thinking.

But when a reader is sucked into a story, he has the rare opportunity to reach the bottom of that whirlpool without dying, he can become a fish, allowing himself to be carried along through those noiseless realms, and when he has seen enough, he can simply shut the book. Of course there are times when a reader sees a favorite thought smashed to pieces by a given text, or when he finds that just as the story has sucked him in, he has also sucked the story into himself, irrevocably (as tends to be the case with suction), so that from that moment on his memory is permeated with what he has read. It's possible that a lot of cold or even foul-smelling air could enter his head that way, because balance is being restored—in this case, from the open eyes of the author who writes the letters on the page to the open eyes of the reader who reads them. Windows and doors slam shut. Even so, a guest is there.

JUNE 2001

In Another World

I sing. My cousin hates it. I chirp, whistle, warble, improvise coloraturas. My best friend hates it. I can't stand that pitch, she says,
but I forget her, and forget myself, and sing. Just like that, for no
one but myself. When I'm feeling good, I sing because I'm feeling good, and when I'm feeling bad, I sing because I'm feeling
bad, when things are hectic, I sing to calm my nerves, and when
I have a lot of time, I just sing. Singing is free, and it belongs to
me. Even as a heathen I join the choir, I sing the hymns and *Re-
joice! Exult!* I do believe, but in what? Probably in the divine wind
and its echo in the Gothic forest, the most beautiful thing I've
ever heard so far. At home my mother asks: Have you practiced
piano yet? I practice piano. One hour a day, because I'm a good
girl. But at night, under the covers, I secretly listen to the week's
pop hits on my small portable radio that's held together with tape
and turned down to a conspiratorial volume, I listen to ABBA
when I'm doing the dishes (I sing along), I dance by myself to
anything at all when there's nobody home, then I put the white
collar back on and head to the choir loft: *For all flesh is as grass, and
all the glory of man as the flower of grass*, the most beautiful thing I've
ever heard, and Friday night dancing close to the last song at the
disco, "Smoke on the Water," and gradually the piano notes are
also transformed into something that isn't made of paper anymore, my obedience turns into freedom, the music that I play
for myself pours over me, I listen to myself, listen to the music
I'm making, I get lost in it, that must be why the Doors are called
the Doors, there are always these doors through the music, doors
that pull me into the world beyond the world, into the moving
air, until I get dizzy, Jim Morrison, a red light bulb hanging in
the bedroom of a friend from school, *and as the first head rolls I'll*

say: hoppla,* and at home I still dance by myself to anything at all, Verdi's apocalypse pours over me, my body belongs to me, and with my first love I come to know Bach and Glenn Gould, the most beautiful thing I've ever heard, and when that love is betrayed Bach and Glenn Gould are proscribed, purged from my rotation as a sort of purification, a painful withdrawal, and I'm always dancing alone, no no, because then along comes someone who says: What, you're dancing alone, I can't stand women like that, so he takes the dancing away, but in return he gives me Gesualdo's sixth book of madrigals, music beyond music, and when I listen to that, I know that now that is really the most beautiful thing I've ever heard, then "Just Don't Cry About Love" again, and Hans Albers singing "Cheerio" after his friend Johnny has died, that has to be the most beautiful thing I've ever heard, I cry out of love and I hear two old women in the countryside singing a duet, *Ohoho you little flea, hop so high and merrily*, I make a recording, a year later the older woman is dead, she's taken the duet to the grave with her, in the meantime I've studied opera, directing, with a hint of longing to switch my focus to singing (I sing), but if I can't sing Isolde then there's no point, her lament for Tristan is certainly the most beautiful thing I've ever heard. And finally, day after day and evening after evening, music please, I say in the opera house, and then the music begins, please, and the Gypsy Princess appears on stage, she bewitches everyone with her voice, but in the hallways backstage I sing (warble, improvise flourishes and coloraturas): *The greatest thing a woman can achieve is surely not to love, but to be loved!* Please. Music is made of waves that touch our flesh, and maybe that's why it disarms me like nothing else. I love, or I listen to music, I don't know exactly where one begins and the other ends. And now I have a child who sits in my kitchen

---

* Bertolt Brecht, *The Threepenny Opera*, trans. Ralph Manheim and John Willett (New York: Bloomsbury, 1979), 21.

and sings and warbles, just like that, who likes listening to music.
And when he listens, he looks as if he's in another world, beyond
the world.

JULY 2005

My Favorite Fairy Tale: "Clever Hans"

Clever Hans, trapped between his bride and his mother.

Hans goes to his bride Gretel and accepts her gifts.

Hans goes back home, and his mother tells him what to do with them.

But he's always just one step behind.

He puts the needle in the haystack, but sticks the knife into his shirtsleeve; he puts the goat into his bag, where it suffocates, but ties the bacon on a rope, where it's eaten by dogs; afterward he puts a calf on his head, and it kicks him in the face—but in the end, when Gretel wants to give herself to him, he ties her up with a rope, leads her to the stall, and tries to feed her hay. "That was ill done, Hans, you should have cast friendly eyes on her," says his mother.[*] So Hans goes into the stall, pokes out the eyes of all of the calves and sheep, and throws them in Gretel's face.

At first Hans is laughable, we laugh at his endless journeys back and forth, at his abundant greed, we laugh at the way that he takes everything literally, and at the fact that Hans himself is always in motion, but his head is so stubbornly resistant to change. Until, in the end, it seems that he has heard our laughter, and all at once his stupidity turns to wickedness, in the end, our laughter has transformed a laughable child into a savage creature. In the end, his mistake has consequences for the world that allowed him to go astray. Is this despair another gift for Hans? Or is it his gift to his bride? Does he drive his mother to despair? Or does she drive him to despair with her tests? Is Hans exhausted by his hunt for the obvious? Or is he, Hans, the

[*] Jacob Grimm and Wilhelm Grimm, *The Complete Grimm's Fairy Tales*, trans. James Stern and Margaret Hunt (New York: Pantheon Books, 1972), 168.

one who exhausts the women with his constant greed? Are the women laughing at him—or are they crying? Does Hans play dumb in order to fight for his freedom? Does he lose or win in the end? Whose side are they on—this laughter, this despair, this exhaustion? The Grimms' tale doesn't say. The mechanics of the tale make me laugh, its savagery appalls me, but the underlying moral isn't given to me, I'm free to choose that for myself. And no one can tell me where Hans's father is.

FEBRUARY 2006

How I Write

I've graduated from the university. I have my diploma, I have a short-term job working three days a week at a bakery, and I'm collecting public assistance. I cook hardboiled eggs and make rolls into sandwiches, I hand children cookies across the counter, arrange pieces of cake on baking sheets, and mop the floor every evening after closing time, twice in a row: the first time wet, to loosen the crumbs, the second time only damp. I've graduated from the university, I'm working three days a week at a bakery, and aside from that I have a lot of time.

I've always written. For my fourteenth birthday, my parents gave me a bright blue typewriter. I didn't study writing, that's not what my degree is in, but it's a part of me, and all I need in order to write is myself, my bright blue typewriter, and time.

I remember the story of something that happened when I was fourteen. It's the story of a girl who isn't really a girl anymore. That's the story that I'm going to write.

It's five in the morning, and I'm standing in front of the mirror, pulling back my hair in a ponytail for the morning shift, when suddenly it occurs to me that I also look like a girl, but I'm not really a girl anymore. So maybe I can even take real life as my material, there's no material as good as real life.

It's late August, time for school to start. I'm twenty-seven, I've graduated from the university, and I finally have time to seek out reality for myself. So I make some phone calls, pay some visits, and within three days I've found a principal who's willing to let me enroll in eleventh grade with a fake name, a fake address, and a fake birthdate, so that I can gather material for my book.

On September 1, I'm standing in front of the class as "the new girl"—and it actually works. Nobody points at me, nobody laughs at me. In a single moment I've gotten ten years younger, and I sit where the teacher tells me to sit. For the next three weeks, I forget that I can drive, forget my boyfriend, forget the university and my job at the bakery. Instead, I learn what a seventeen-year-old's handwriting looks like, learn to say my fake name, learn that I can be as dumb as I want, since my grades will have no real consequences. I pack my binder before I go to bed, I carry blue and red folders that slowly grow dog-eared, I have to raise my hand when I want to speak in class, and in gym class I'm embarrassed by my adult body. Whenever someone asks me what I want to be when I grow up, I say: I don't know yet. When we take tests, I help the girl next to me, but I earn an F myself and it doesn't phase me. I'm as free as an angel, because at the end of these three weeks, when my notebook is full of reality, I can just leave school again.

After that, I work at the bakery again, three days a week, I cook hardboiled eggs and make rolls into sandwiches, I hand children cookies across the counter, arrange pieces of cake on baking sheets, and mop the floor every evening after closing time. In my free time, I work on my story about a woman who doesn't want to grow up.

NOVEMBER 2006

63

Among People

I've never given an acceptance speech before, I've never had to give one—that's because this Solothurn Prize is the first time I've hit the jackpot, so to speak. I've come within a hair of winning some prizes, or gotten second place, if there was a second place—I was always surprised that I'd even made it to the short-list, sometimes I agreed with the jury's decision, which made it easy to accept defeat, but sometimes the prize didn't go to me or to the person I would have given it to—in those cases I had the feeling that the jury hadn't been able to agree and had decided instead on a candidate who met with less resistance. Of course I very much hope that in this case I wasn't the candidate who met with the least resistance, but the one the whole jury agreed on!

What does it mean, then, for me to win this prize? It means that what I wrote—the thoughts and feelings that I translated into letters—was capable of being translated back into thoughts and feelings by readers, it means that I'm not alone with the baggage of life, it also means that the insoluble equations, the questions that I pass along to my readers, are questions that I no longer have to work away at on my own, it means that we, my readers and I, will divide the work among ourselves. It also means that some of my descriptions struck solid ground, struck something like the blue clay in my last book, *Visitation*, a layer deeper than anything can grow, a layer that lets no water seep through. Struck something that can be reached with the emotions, but not penetrated, the essential thing.

Does a prize change anything about the work? Does it make writing easier? In one respect it certainly does: For a while, you don't have to worry about mere survival, you don't have to be careful to send in the grant applications by the deadline, you can let your mind wander, and you don't have to be ready, as soon as one book appears in print, to turn in the first twenty pages of the next book, a book that's hardly even ready for your own eyes. You don't have to take on jobs just to earn money, jobs that take up space in your mind, you can stay home and think in peace.

Unfortunately, though, in other respects a prize doesn't change anything about writing: When you write something down that has to be thought through first, the thinking is still hard, you start at the very beginning each time, and each time you're entirely on your own. The brief signal from parallel worlds provides some pleasure in the present, but for the writing that remains to be done in the future, it unfortunately doesn't offer any help. To be sure, it gives you some confidence that you "can write," as they say, but the impossibilities that compel you to write remain impossibilities, despite your outward success. And being able to write is also a matter of luck as soon as you find yourself sitting alone at your desk again. Unfortunately, my doubts can't be assuaged from outside. Every time I start a new work, I ask myself the same questions, ask myself if I've ever really known how to write down a sentence—just one to start with—how to look at a story, how it's even possible to turn the innermost things outward, and then, after stripping off my own skin, to peer through it. Each time, I've found that I don't know anymore.

Recently the chairman of the jury, Hans Ulrich Probst, called me to ask if I had any requests for the processional and recessional music at this prize ceremony, and the newspaper editor at the *Mittelland Zeitung* wrote to tell me when he would need the text of my acceptance speech so that it could be published. It's been three weeks to the day since I sat in the funeral home to discuss my mother's funeral, and the woman from the funeral home asked me if I had any requests for the processional and recessional music at the service, and what I would like to do about the speech—if it would be too hard for me to deliver it myself, she could recommend a good speaker.

The one speech is a speech for life and in the midst of life, it is a speech of thanks for the fact that some people find value in my work, an expression of hope that this exchange of questions and answers between me and my readers will continue for a while, as long as I am in this world. The other speech is a speech for my mother, in the midst of death, it is a reminder of my mother, and my own affirmation that from now on I will have to be content with what we had, forever. That farewell is integrated into our lives just like the other ceremony: With processional and recessional music, death is integrated into life through the ritual that the living know. But when the two coincide so closely, as they have done in this moment of my life, as closely as life and nothingness coincide in the moment of death, then they are reflected in one another, they shake hands, and for a moment they exchange sides.

Thank you very much.

JUNE 2008

On "The Old Child"

When they found her, she was standing on the street with an empty bucket in one hand, on a street lined with shops, and didn't say a word. When she was brought to the police station, all the official questions were put to her: What her name was, where she lived, her parents, her age. The girl replied that she was fourteen years old, but she couldn't tell them her name, nor where her home was. At first, the policemen had called the girl "miss," but now they stopped. They said: How can you not know where you came from, where you were before you stood on the street here with your empty bucket? The girl simply could not remember, she couldn't remember the beginning. She was an orphan through and through, and all she had, all she knew was the empty bucket she held in one hand and continued to hold as the policemen questioned her. One of the men tried to insult the girl, saying: Scraping the bottom of the bucket, eh? But the girl didn't even notice that his words were meant to give offense, she replied simply: Yes.

So the old child was standing on the street at night, standing with an empty bucket in her hand on a street lined with shops, and she didn't say a word.

And now I'm standing here on a podium for the first time to give a lecture, and I'm supposed to say something. What's *my* empty bucket?

My faulty memory, the lost GDR, the secrets that I want to keep to myself?

When I tell you that I had a very different childhood than

All translations of *Geschichte vom alten Kind* are quoted from Jenny Erpenbeck, *The Old Child & Other Stories*, trans. Susan Bernofsky (New York: New Directions, 2005).

this old child must have had—assuming that this child existed at all—does that tell you anything? Does that mean that I'm hiding behind a character who's very different from the person I am, or was? And aren't we allowed to hide ourselves in literature? Do we actually have to pour our heart and soul into it, as they say? Pour it all out so explicitly that every single person understands that this really is our so-called heart and soul?

Or isn't writing always a kind of translation, when it comes down to it?

When I say on the first page of the book that the child doesn't say anything, that doesn't mean that the child just keeps quiet. It means that she's decided to say nothing. Not speaking is just as much a statement as speaking. It is the hollow form of speech.

When the bucket is empty, that means that *everything* that might have been inside or could have been inside is now contained in that emptiness. In that sense the empty bucket is closer to the truth than a half-full one.

In my first draft of this lecture, I thought I had to try to say a lot. I thought I had to tell you about myself, about my childhood in peacetime, which was very different from my parents' childhood during and after the war, about the one year I was allowed to spend in Rome when I was seven, a notable exception to the rule, about my youth in peacetime, about literature and music, about learning bookbinding, about the fall of the wall. But it isn't always the case—in fact it's probably only rarely the case—that saying more brings us closer to the truth than saying less. What we say is always a selection, and no matter how loudly we speak, the things that we conceal quietly persist in their concealed existence. After all, what do we know about the spongy sea monsters that may have been squeezing themselves into the deepest, darkest trenches of some ocean or other for the past two hundred years? We don't know much about them, and it's the same with other people, we only know what's floating on the surface, in fact we probably don't know much more about ourselves than the things we've told other people so many times that we've finally begun to believe them. When we talk a lot, we have to be careful not to get lost in the vortex of anecdotes, not to put ourselves at the mercy of the same stories that we tell over and over.

As an author, I know a little bit about the character in my book; if nothing else, I know that she's holding an empty bucket in her hand. And I also know what she plans to do: to lie about her age, to make herself young. But that's all I know, and all I need to know.

At readings, people often ask me why there's no information about the character's backstory. They seem to think that I know this backstory, that I'm concealing it. But in fact this character's backstory doesn't matter, even to me.

Before I started writing the story of the old child, of course, I had thought about which part of the story I should tell. That may be the hardest question to answer for any story. It's not just a matter of what interests you, it's also a matter of what sort of space takes shape beyond the part that you tell. It's a question of what need not, or cannot, be said. The part that isn't told takes on great power, if you look at the story from the right perspective, often even greater power than the part that's revealed. As paradoxical as it may seem: The untold side of a story can weigh even heavier in a reader's mind than its twin, the hollow form of a story that is actually told. This preponderance of one of the two sides—sides which actually ought to correspond (*correspond*) to one another—may result from the fact that the half of the story that's told allows the reader to remain ensconced within it, but the half of the story that's untold requires the reader to be constantly aware of the fact that it remains untold, whether he wants to or not. Therefore, even while the reader constructs some concrete untold story for himself out of the story that is told—even while he imagines a "real," more or less comprehensible story—he never forgets that the untold half, the story that he has only imagined, is a story that could not be spoken, could not be written, for one reason or another—therefore he regards this speechless part from inside and outside at the same time, and that is probably why the concealed part carries so much weight.

Let us consider what options I might have had when it comes to taking the real events that occurred and turning them into a "plot." What kind of stories I might have written, based on the same facts.

What happened is this: A grown woman posed as a fourteen-year-old child and spent some time in a children's home. We don't know why she decided to undertake this experiment. We also don't know how she managed to infiltrate the children's home. We don't know what kind of family she came from. We know that she was able to maintain the illusion that she was a child for at least a few months, she even fooled people her own age, so apparently she really did look like a child. We know that she wrote letters, and that those letters, too, created a convincing impression that they had been written by a child, right down to the handwriting. We know that the woman got sick, and that a medical examination revealed that she *had* to be an adult. We know that she was subsequently admitted to the psychiatric ward of a hospital.

So, what kinds of stories could be made out of this incident?

If you'd prefer something light-hearted, we all know what that story looks like—it's been made into a film called *The Punch Bowl*. Today it might even be made into a fantasy film.

Or maybe the woman would only be a schoolgirl by day and an adult by night, a sort of Lolita-meets-Ms.-Jekyll-and-Ms.-Hyde.

But if we wanted it to be erotic, for example, we could make it a story about a woman, disguised as a "stray child," who hides behind her childlike face to infiltrate the family of her lover. Then her lover would have a real problem on his hands.

However, we could also make our theme something like *this*: We could tell the story of a woman who loses her desire to live as an adult as a consequence of some horrible event—perhaps abuse, perhaps rape, perhaps the death of her parents—and who decides that she wants to return to her childhood, to that "idyllic" life. Then the book would end with the scene where my own *Old Child* begins. Then the last sentence would be: "When they asked her who her parents were, her age, she only replied that she was fourteen years old."

Julia Franck chose a similar conceit for her book *The Blindness of the Heart*. There she tells the story of a mother who simply leaves her eight-year-old son on a train platform one day and disappears forever. Julia Franck introduces this event at the beginning of the book, but then spends the entire book recounting the backstory, saving the main character's momentous decision for the end. The unusual thing in this case is that for all its detail, the backstory doesn't explain the event.

In Walter Kempowski's novel *All for Nothing*, which is set in East Prussia shortly before the end of the Second World War, this is even more clearly the case, the actual story lies in the discrepancy between the book and its ending. Kempowski first constructs an entire universe of biographies and fates in meticulous detail, only to annihilate this universe in the course of just a few lines at the end of the book (and of the war), so that ultimately— through circumstances that are only roughly sketched out, and that are fundamentally banal—the characters we have followed throughout the course of the book all meet their deaths. What makes this book so devastating is the fact that it is *not* possible to make any sense of this ending—given that there has to be an ending—from the scrupulously narrated account. We are shaken by the destruction of a world which, until this war began, had seemed to conform to intelligible principles of cause and effect. As this book clearly shows, the perspective always *is* the story.

To return to my own story, *The Old Child*, even if we selected exactly the same portion of the story that I chose—beginning on the day when the girl / woman arrives at the children's home—the story could still be a very different one. For instance, if the character who stepped onstage were not a shapeless creature whose own flesh served as a disguise, but perhaps an aging nymphet, a treacherous, pretty floozy who could outdo all of the other children at being a child, conjuring up a second youth for herself—which would probably be more fun than getting a facelift.

Or, if you insist, we could tell the story of a human rights activist who infiltrates an East German children's home to study the ideological underpinnings of early education.

Ultimately, we could try it all at once: start with the troubled years of the girl's actual childhood, then follow her through her second, voluntary childhood in the children's home, and then continue even beyond that, into the real adulthood of this would-be girl. (But that probably would have made for a much thicker book.) In that case, it would have been a book divided into three parts, a book that keeps transforming itself—Schlink's *The Reader* is one example of a book like that, where the story in which we have become invested keeps transforming itself into a very different story.

And so on and so forth.

But what we actually make out of our "material" fundamentally depends not only on the possibilities inherent in that material, but also on which of those possibilities set our own thoughts in motion, intersecting with our own life stories and experiences, however indirectly.

Is it the possibility of transformation that makes the story of such an "old child" so alluring? The theme of time travel? Is it the theme of becoming an adult, or in this case, of not wanting to become an adult? Is it the fraud that the story entails? The disgrace? The question of what identity is, or how others perceive it? The question of self-fashioning? The game? Or the question of what an adult does with the freedom that children lack? Of course this is also a story about power—"Knowledge is power," as every East German child learned in school—a story about deception as power, about knowledge withheld, about manipulation, it is about what can be said even if it might not be true, and what must remain unsaid. It is about the lack of certainty in our conversations with one another, about who is using whom, what stories we tell ourselves with our own lives, and what stories we tell others. It is about the broad spectrum between guilt and innocence, perhaps also about revenge, about weakness as a mask worn to mislead the strong, about vanities placed on display, and the question of how many layers terms like "victim" and "perpetrator" must be filtered through before they even begin to make sense. It is quite clearly about the search for one's own path, and consequently about going astray as well, and of course on a quite fundamental level it is about the circumstances under which the main character makes her decision to exchange one world for another. About this world that becomes visible only through the actions of the main character, just as a chemical dissolved in a clear liquid becomes visible only when it precipitates out.

So how should we approach this story: from the perspective of depth psychology, of fantasy, of politics?

In any case, you can see that this story is full of possibilities, and that's what makes it a good story, even before it is written. Unfortunately, though, the book doesn't exist before it is written, the author would be left standing there empty-handed. Or maybe with her hands full? After all, as we've just seen, everything is already there in principle, albeit only as a possibility to begin with. The empty bucket, the full one.

In my first draft of this lecture, I wanted to try to show how the experiences I had had in my life before I was 27 years old had condensed—like water in a giant cloud—and then finally rained down as the words of my first book. *The transformation of a quantity into a new quality* is one of the basic principles of dialectics. Maybe it's just that I've been asked too many times whether this or that story that I tell is autobiographical—so that now, in an act of premature obedience, I wanted to present you with the recipe for my first book.

Of course there has to be a life that has condensed, that has accumulated, and of course at some point there has to be an impulse, a vision of the intimate connection you can enter into with such a story, there has to be an intuitive knowledge, not yet present in words, that this particular story will lead you into spaces that you want to, or have to, enter. There must be a point of entry, one that is unfamiliar but nonetheless leads you into yourself. But it's not as if I could just say: these particular parents, these particular experiences of happiness or unhappiness, of games, of lies, of parallel worlds, of West and East. As if you could just enter all of those data and then this exact book would come out.

Recently I searched for a name online. And because I'm forgetful, I searched for the same name in the same search engine a few days later. The search results were different. It was just like my father always used to tell me: There's an element of disorder, something intractable, in every order, things have a life of their own even if they appear predictable. The same data won't always produce the same results. The same or similar experiences produce a different book in the head of every writer (if they produce one at all). And even if two authors had exactly the same ideas about the "plot," they'd still end up with two different books, because a book is always something encrypted, something like a secret code: a mask that you put on so that you can run naked through the soccer stadium without being recognized. And each person would put on a different mask, since there are always complex experiences at play in the decision to run naked across a soccer field, experiences that go beyond this or that particular story.

Recently someone told me that every language has its own sign language. A missed opportunity, I thought at first, but then I was simply amazed. So even in the domain of gestures and facial expressions, it is impossible to find a universal language. Most people in the world walk, talk, sleep, eat, drink, love, and fight, but still the gestures for walking, sleeping, eating, drinking, loving, and fighting that deaf people use in English are different from the gestures for walking, sleeping, eating, drinking, loving, and fighting used in Greek, Russian, or Chinese.

The world is there in every word, no matter how small. The world is poured into each of these literary words as into a funnel, which draws together all of the writer's life circumstances and experiences, everything the writer knows, and possibly hates, about culture and history, but also about vegetation, landscape, climate, the sense of time, and other elements of the writer's surroundings, incorporating them into a single stream. Because literary writing is always, at the same time, an act of translation, condensing everything you know, everything you have experienced, into a few words—and the writer's choice of words always depends upon all the countless other stories that have been poured into those words, on the charges the words carry, on the world that has called them forth.

Of course, there are always sentences, even if you're not writing a book.

For instance, if someone asks me about the fall of the wall today, I can describe my situation at the time more or less like this:

I didn't want to go "across." Across the border, just like that. To have my ID card stamped at one of those laminate tables that had been set up as a provisional measure and then take a look at the West. I needed time. I didn't want to let myself get dragged along with the tide. Until that moment, my country had existed for itself, and we lived among ourselves, no one on the outside cared what we thought, so we were free to think in peace and quiet, it was strangely peaceful and quiet, we could peacefully and quietly get worked up about this, that, and the other thing, peacefully and quietly file complaints, peacefully and quietly hope that Honecker would step down soon, but we weren't a wonder to ourselves, we were the everyday world, and in that everyday world we were among ourselves. We may have been provincial in comparison to the economy of the West, but we were the avant-garde when it came to believing in a bright future, even if it would only become a reality long after our own lifetimes. So long after our own lifetimes that it was worth settling in for a long wait. Isolated as in a laboratory, we were occupied with our own mistakes and the mistakes of our government, but that meant that we had long since moved beyond the mistakes of the old world; the only thing that connected us to the big wide world outside was international solidarity, the worldwide struggle for the release of Luis Corvalán or Angela Davis; as children we had translated these grand efforts into very manageable forms, like bake sales or recycling drives, donating all of the proceeds to the cause. Sheltered, perhaps. But the sheltered life in East Germany also meant that there was no pornography; yet there were plenty of naked people right in the middle of Berlin, sunbathing on the grass in Weinbergspark. Berlin was a capital city, but those infernal terms like "desirable location" were still foreign to us, because all of East Berlin lay outside of the world in which desirable locations existed. Idyll. Innocence. Indecency. Inbreeding. My parents' furniture was in the Biedermeier style, and our money was light like play money. So I could certainly talk about the fall of the wall—and if someone asked me about my feelings at the time, I would say something like: It dragged us into this big, wide world so quickly that there was no time to think. Did it drag us forward or backward? Backward, I felt. Only after several weeks of refusal did I set foot in that foreign land that spoke the same language, even the same Berlin dialect, only then did I cross the border for the first time. A door that only opens once a century had opened, but now that century was gone forever. Something was going too quickly, going wrong, I felt. If nothing else, the skeptical attitude that we had cultivated toward our own government had taught us once and for all to keep a critical distance, to maintain our independent thinking in light of the government's flawed stewardship of our common goal. None of my friends believed that the world in which we had lived was the best of all possible worlds—but now, all of a sudden, we were supposed to believe that that best of all possible worlds had been found? There was a lot of talk of *freedom* now, but I couldn't make much of this word *freedom*, which floated freely in all sorts of sentences. *Freedom* to travel? (But will we be able to afford it?) Or *freedom* of opinion? (What if no one cares about my opinion?) *Freedom* to shop? (But what happens when we're finished shopping?)

Freedom wasn't given freely, it came at a price, and the price was my entire life up to that point. The price was that everything that had been called the present up until then was suddenly called the past. The majority had defeated the minority and done away with socialism, and the minority, which believed in the continued existence of a socialist system, in improvements, replacements, wasn't even asked anymore, freedom was suddenly freedom of the majority.

And if anyone wants to know what the biggest difference was, in my view, between my old life and my new life, I'd say something like this: Suddenly we, who had been alone with ourselves until that point, were being measured by the world's standards. And suddenly "the world" meant anyplace with a stronger economy. Suddenly. Suddenly our speech, too, was being judged by the world's standards, like a language of the ancient Orient whose symbols can still be deciphered, even though the world that produced them has been buried for all time. Because suddenly our everyday lives weren't everyday lives anymore, they were a museum, or an adventure to be recounted, our customs were an attraction. In the course of just a few weeks, what had been self-evident ceased to be self-evident.

Today I can speak in sentences like these, but even today it's difficult.

These sentences describe a particular state of affairs concretely and straightforwardly, but if someone asks where they come from, they can only keep silent.

That's why sentences like these aren't always enough.

Sentences like these are like the small part of a glacier that can be seen protruding above the surface of the water, while the glacier's much larger, lower body remains submerged, silent and unseen. How, then, should I talk about a feeling that not even I can access in my own thoughts, let alone someone who has only heard the few sentences that can be spoken.

People who think that they speak the same language that I do, namely German, will respond to these sentences, these sentences will be attacked, doubted, discussed. But there can be no discussion of experiences and feelings. They have their own, wholly individual morality, and they lie beyond the knowledge that we later acquire. They are simply there.

And so these sentences look like sentences that can be understood, but in truth they cannot be understood.

People will laugh about them.

People will say that they're the wrong sentences.

And yet I can't use any other sentences, as long as I *speak*.

Still, I can keep quiet, I don't have to say them, that's why I always turn down invitations to take part in discussions of the so-called "turn," the reunification. By the way, it's interesting to consider whether this silence is actually freedom. But let's set the word "freedom" aside for now.

So you could keep quiet.

But you could also write.

If the language that you can speak isn't enough, that's a very good reason to start writing. As paradoxical as it may be: The impossibility of expressing what happens to us in words is what pushes us toward writing. Whenever I have *not* been able to understand something, have *not* been able to capture it in words, that's when I've started writing. And that's how it was with my first book, too.

I remember that it took about a year from the time I decided to write the book until I actually started writing it. It was the year that I directed an opera, the final step in earning my degree in opera directing. 1993–94. I still remember very clearly how after I finished my degree, I suddenly had nothing to do but work half days at the bakery and spend the rest of my time actually writing this book, the task I'd set for myself. The GDR hadn't taught me how to be unemployed.

Only at that moment did I experience a sort of virginal amazement at the fact that a book isn't there until you write it. If I don't make the girl appear, she doesn't appear. If I don't make her think, keep quiet, say something now and then, meet this or that person, then she doesn't think, doesn't keep quiet, doesn't say anything, doesn't meet anyone. Then there's no girl, and no story.

And yet the story wasn't even there in my head yet either, at least not in the sense that I could simply write it down.

Yes, there is a field there that is beckoning (indeed, many important scenes in the theater take place in an "open field"), but the story isn't there yet. Woyzeck hunts for mushrooms at night in an open field, it's more or less like that. So I make my way across the field, blind and seeing at the same time. *Groping* would probably be a better way to express it, the way that I try to conjure up something that isn't even there yet, to make it materialize out of a blind spot; my search leads me out, that is, I lead myself—but the reverse is also true, as it is in every search, I'm led by the thing I'm searching for. So it's a state in between the knowledge that something is there and the ignorance of what that something is. This, I think, is what makes the work of writing so much like love, makes it exert a pull on us like love. By the way, this process of groping is also the reason that sentences which may be false in their own right can still be true, because the field that I make my way across as I write can only be partly comprehended by the understanding.

With this first book—in which a young woman pretends to be a child and has herself committed to a children's home so that she doesn't have to be an adult—I began my adult life. I had my first experiences with the power and powerlessness of writing: the power to decide what should be there on paper, and powerlessness in the face of what wants to and needs to be there. My old child, too, is powerful and powerless at the same time, a victim of her biography, a perpetrator of her false identity. She has plans, but she also has her own retrospective blindness.

So when I write: *she was standing on the street at night with an empty bucket in one hand, on a street lined with shops, and didn't say a word*, then she's standing on a street lined with shops at night, with an empty bucket in her hand, and doesn't say a word. I could also have her appear during the day, in a bustling shopping arcade, or I could have her ring the doorbell at the children's home, or lie on a park bench in the snow, nearly freezing to death before she's found. I'm free to choose (freedom!)—and yet I have to decide, because if everything remains free, then there's no book. But when I write something down, I know that certain ideas will be "kindled" in every reader's imagination, so I have power not only over my character, but also over my reader. For one brief moment, I can decide what path the reader's imagination will follow, even if, as we all know, a different story takes shape in every reader's head, because the words written in the book, and the associations that each reader has with those words—and of course also the circumstances under which the reader reads—will come together to form a different text each time. The street lined with shops will always be a street lined with shops, but it will look a little different in each reader's mind. What it will look like, I don't know. And I don't even know who will read the text that I'm currently working on. So I know that I have a certain power, but I don't know over whom.

But why does the girl have to have *a wide, blotchy face that looks like a moon with shadows on it . . . , broad shoulders like a swimmer's*, etc.?

All right. I want to hide behind the girl, she's my mask, as you know, the mask I wear so that I can run naked across the playing field. So the girl can't look like me. And she can't act as I would act. While I turn a smiling face to the world, a face that always makes me look younger than I really am, while people give me friendly advice because they think I need it, while things come easily to me because people aren't afraid of me—the girl has to be uncouth and unshapely, dirty where I'm clean, timid where

I'm confident, uptight where I'm uninhibited, weak where I'm strong, but nevertheless this girl is *my* mask, nevertheless this girl still has to accept advice when someone thinks she needs it, she can't make others afraid, she has to be able to be happy. And the reverse is true, too: I also have to be uncouth, unshapely, dirty, timid, uptight, and weak. Because otherwise I wouldn't know this character well enough to wear her as a mask. The mask has to fit me but nevertheless hide me, the story has to be my story but still someone else's, if I'm going to be able to tell it at all. That's why Josef Winkler can write in his book *Roppongi*: "When my father died, we were staying in Japan . . . , we drove from To-kyo into the mountains of Nagano, past smoking volcanoes, to a literature symposium," but the Josef Winkler in the book isn't identical to the writer Josef Winkler; and Thomas Bernhard can write in his book *A Child*: "At the age of eight I rode my first few yards on a bicycle in the street below our apartment in the Taubenmarkt in Traunstein. It was midday, and the streets of the self-important little provincial town were empty."* And the eight-year-old child is not identical with the child that Thomas Bernhard, the author of the book, was, because of course it's also possible to wear a mask that shows your own face.

Surely it's a question of the state of matter in which you find yourself, in which you *must* find yourself, when you begin to write. Personally I've always written the texts that mattered most to me, even important letters, on my typewriter, so that I can't recognize myself by my handwriting, so to speak. Writing requires a certain disinhibition, and it's easier to achieve that disinhibition if you're someone else. It requires speed, like breaking into a gallop, and it requires a certain perspective, the right

* Thomas Bernhard, *Gathering Evidence: A Memoir*, trans. David McLintock (New York: Knopf, 1985), 3.

82

eye level—and all of those are borders that can only be surpassed and overcome with the help of courage and desire, the very inverse of fear and shame. But the catalyst for this change of state is surely something that I haven't even mentioned yet: the game.

Even the things that happen in the story of the old child can be described as a game, an experiment. Remember what the so-called "people" chanted when the wall fell: *No more experiments.* The people had had enough of the sandbox game of socialism. The people finally wanted to grow up. But my girl doesn't begin to play until the game is already over:

There must have been a time when the girl, too, thought of a bad grade as something bad, but this time is long past. Meanwhile she has learned that school is the place where errors must occur so as to give it meaning, school is the place of correction, and no bad grade has any real consequences, grades are utterly removed from reality, they stand for the contents of a head, something invisible. And when the teachers then insist that learning is something one does not for school but for Life, this serves only to reinforce the girl's faith that school and Life are two separate things. All that can happen to her here . . . is that the teacher will eventually give up on her, he will be unable to help noticing that the girl's capacity to forget is greater than her capacity to store in her head the subject matter of an eighth-grade class—mathematics, for instance—which would allow her and her head to advance to a ninth-grade classroom at the appointed time. And while the prospect of not being allowed to pass to the next grade might fill the others with terror, implying as it does an additional year of captivity, for the girl it would be a coup. Just as she gives the subject matter its freedom back by forgetting it, she, too, would like to gain her freedom by having the teachers say: This one you can forget about.

Only the girl herself knows the rules of the game that she's playing, her experiment is a lonely one. But like every game, this one too creates another view of the world, evaluating the world from a perspective from which it isn't usually seen. For the girl, it's desirable to occupy the lowest position in the hierarchy, not the highest one that everyone else wants, because the lowest position is the only secure one, precisely because no one wants it. For the girl, it's lovely to be in a children's home, locked in, required to follow certain rules, because in return she gets a place to sleep and enough food to eat, and she doesn't have to worry about a thing. The girl sees the repetitive daily routines in the children's home as a sort of eternity; she sees the revulsion with which others view her as an expression of affection, and by making herself powerless, she gains the power of observation; she looks kindly upon the teachers who want to teach her how things are in life, well aware that they're only playing the roles that she herself has assigned them. In her game, the girl writes herself letters to which she also responds, she leads a monadic life, a life in which she is several people at once, and thus always circles back upon herself. Thus on the one hand she is the girl with a past who has herself committed to the children's home, but on the other hand she is also the girl in the home who has no past, she is one student among others, she is the daughter of a woman she invents for herself, and at the same time she is that woman, and of course she is also, necessarily, the daughter of a real mother and a real father, though we learn nothing about them. She takes refuge in her game, and yet it *is* a game, and the more it becomes a game, the more seriously it demands to be taken, as a response to something that must have actually occurred in the girl's past, something that was not a game.

Conversely—and this point is not without its relevance to the games that many teenagers now play, both on their computers *and* in the real world at the same time—the girl thereby succeeds in undermining the so-called "seriousness" of the world, by interpreting the world as a game. Something similar occurs in the wonderful film *Life is Beautiful*, by the Italian actor, author, and director Roberto Benigni: The father explains the horrific reality of a concentration camp to his son as a game, so that his son will obey the fascists' barbaric rules just for fun, will have fun doing it, and thus—perhaps—will survive.

The girl in my book also strips the world of its seriousness by covering it with a transparent film that transforms the "seriousness of life" into a game, and it doesn't matter if a particular detail of that game might strike the reader as barbaric and distressing, because as long as the girl makes her own rules, she has deprived the world of its power, she is strong, she is *fundamentally* capable of transforming the unbearable into something bearable, and the difficult into something easy.

Lastly, of course, I play a role as well, since when I write a book I write a book *to myself*. I undertake the experiment of responding to some particular things that actually occurred in my own past by looking at reality once again in my own way, reading it anew by describing it according to rules that only I know—rules that I invent anew from moment to moment. In a book, I can describe matters that relate to the same silent, submerged lower body of the glacier that I spoke of earlier, but which appear very different in their details from anything I have experienced myself, and which are thus immeasurably easier for me to articulate. Even if certain details within the reality of the book appear barbaric and distressing, then, it doesn't hurt me, as long as it's only a translation of whatever may actually be troubling me.

But at the same time, of course, the process of writing goes far beyond this sort of translation. Even as I write the story, it begins to pull away from me—to take on a life of its own. I invent the game, and then I lose myself in it. Writing is always an experiment, too, a process with an uncertain outcome and with any number of meanings that aren't necessarily clear to me as the writer while I am writing, perhaps these meanings even penetrate more deeply when I am not aware of them. Every text is, fundamentally, an attempt at a text.

If I want to know whether it might be appropriate for me to insert dreams here and there, I can try it. I test it out, make a collage, so to speak, and then I look at it, I ask myself if it's appropriate for the girl to articulate her identity as an "I" in these few, subconscious moments.

Or I knock the last line of one paragraph against the first line of the next and listen to the sound they make. For instance:

The girl and the boy with greasy hair are locked together with a bicycle lock on the playground, the girl is also forced to bend over, because she's taller than the boy with greasy hair. The last sentence of this paragraph reads:

The girl and the boy with greasy hair have to stand there listening as the dry leaves of the chestnut trees tumble to the ground.

The first sentence of the next paragraph reads:

The weight of my life is increasing.

Now we all know that the dry leaves of a chestnut tree are light, so the weight, the heaviness must be of a different kind, the heaviness here stems from the condition of dryness, of being past the prime of life. And then as this paragraph (which is one of those that recount the girl's dreams) continues, we also hear about the house of Baba Yaga, the witch from Russian fairy tales, whose house sits on a giant hen's foot. But for the girl in my story this house is made of straw, and there is talk of a storm that could apparently set this straw "witch's palace" on fire. The last sentence of this paragraph is: *It [the palace] will make a beautiful bonfire.*

As the writer—a position which naturally makes me the first reader, too—I suddenly hear the dry burning of the witch's straw palace, together with the dry rustling sound of the falling chestnut leaves. And now, we come to the first sentence of the next paragraph. It goes like this:

The girl knows that her body is a transgression, she would like to atone for it, and so she obeys the decrees issued by her classmates to the letter.

In the space between the previous paragraph and this one, we can now hear what actually happens. We have the crackling, we have a burning palace of straw (perched atop a chicken's foot), and now we also have the delinquent, whose sinful body is being burned upon a pyre.

All of this results from the way that these sentences knock against one another, and from the empty spaces in between the sentences. By the way, I had to fight for those empty spaces— first with my own publisher and later in some of the translations, too—because it wasn't always clear that a line left free of words isn't a waste of paper just because there's nothing printed there, it's a line left free.

Of course, while I'm actually writing, these thoughts don't all run through my mind in the way that I've just laid them out for you, I don't express them in complete sentences for myself in the way that I've just done for you, I don't calculate the effect to be achieved by a certain arrangement of paragraphs; instead I just listen for some consonance between them, and I'm glad when I find it there—I shy away from thinking *through* everything that takes place between lines like that, thinking it through to its conclusion; even while I'm working to ensure the truth of the text itself, I'm thinking around the truth, so to speak, probably out of fear that this truth could disappear if I were to look it in the face or speak its name. After all, the Swan Knight in Wagner's *Lohengrin* must also depart again after his wife asks him his name. So it's important to leave the text some space for itself, but I'll return to that point later.

As horrible as some of the individual incidents that I depict may be, then, it's still always a pleasure to view an entire world through unfamiliar eyes. In the winter, when the other children in the home are freezing and running around in the slush, I can make the girl blossom, and I can send her to the hospital in the spring, when the others are having their first experiences with love. In this way, I can read the entire world and the cycle of a year in reverse, I can filter the world through various layers, and then for brief moments I can look through all of these layers at once, as if looking down from the elevated Platform 12 to the underground Platform 3 in Berlin Central Station. For instance, here we have the cycle of the year, the girl's fake age, the history of Germany in the 20th century, an elderly mother who can't be a mother at all, a sort of primal mother, like Erda in German mythology. We can see the National Socialists' ambitions for total domination reflected in the girl's self-abasement, and we can see the destruction of Dresden, which is mentioned at one point, as a sign of the failure of those ambitions, the nearing end; at the very moment when the girl falls down, when she seems to have finally become a child in reality, I can make her pass through this resounding success and come out the other side, on the side of failure, because her resounding success turns out to be the beginning of an illness that will bring her false identity to light. Success suddenly transmutes into failure, which naturally raises the question of whether we ever truly arrive at the goals that we reach.

But since I studied opera directing, I could also sneak in a line from a work like the *Rosenkavalier*, and then the whole thing would have been *a masquerade, and nothing more*, recalling the Marschallin's monologue about the unfathomable passage of time.

Or I could translate the Mandelbrot set into the walks taken by my old child; the Mandelbrot set is the graphic representation of complex numbers and their relationships to one another, an astonishingly clear visual demonstration of the fact that all relationships repeat themselves and are contained within each other, only on different scales.

I can leave clues in a book as in a child's game, as in a treasure hunt, and it doesn't even make a difference at first whether the reader—if there ever is a reader—finds the clue or not, because *my* game consists in creating the mere possibility for it to be found. Remember, as long as there's an empty bucket, the full bucket is always contained within it. So my book is my game, and like every game it's very much alive. And especially when I'm alone, or can't speak, or don't want to speak, or when no one speaks my language with me, a book is always also an opportunity to remain in dialogue, just as every solitary game is a mild form of schizophrenia.

Before I come to an end, I'd like to return again to the question of why my character *doesn't concern* me. When I was talking about writing as an attempt to make a collage out of various materials, I mentioned that the last and first lines of successive paragraphs produce a certain concordance, that they organize themselves, like particles in a magnetic field, around a kernel of truth that I don't *want* to think through all the way to its conclusion. I try not to name what's at the center of this field, *you should never ask me*, and the "old child" doesn't give her own name, not even a fake name. I don't know her real name either, or her fake name, she remains nameless amidst so many Maiks and Nicoles. The things that a character like that doesn't want to say, or can't, that she doesn't want to disclose, that she would prefer to keep quiet, those things tell us something about that character. We find, too, that the place that the girl chooses—the children's home—is a no-place, a blank spot on the map of the real world, and this, too, tells us something about the character. The home is supposed to prepare children for life outside, but it has its own life: its own grounds, its own rules, its own time. So the girl, who is actually already an adult, goes down the wrong path, she goes off-track, she wraps herself in a cocoon, and of course the way that she withdraws into herself and into these tightly constrictive surroundings also manifests certain symptoms of illness, of disturbed communication. But if we look at it from the other side, the girl finds her own way to get what she needs in order to be an adult, to develop some sort of consciousness of herself. Above all, she asserts her freedom from the constraints of adult life, she slows down her own development, she takes her time.

So a border is a restriction, but it also creates a protected space for experimentation. Within that border, as long as it holds, something fragile can begin to grow; on the other hand a border like that is also in its very nature the sign of a tension between inside and outside, and in this sense it contains the possibility of its own dissolution, the possibility that the pressure differential that has built up between these two temporarily separated systems will be balanced out. The time that the girl spends in the home is a form of escape, but as the end of the story reveals, it may also be a period of preparation. A chance to catch up on childhood on her own terms, and perhaps, after her illness and the resulting revelation of her true identity, this will finally lead to a real adult life.

When I started writing this story, I had a degree in opera directing and little chance of getting a full-time job in an opera house, even as a director's assistant, let alone as a director. I was working at *John's* bakery in Pankow, nicely arranging pieces of cake on baking sheets so that people would still buy them even when we were about to close, and when I wasn't working at the bakery, I traveled around in the world and took my first little laptop with me to write. I didn't write the book because I wanted to become a writer. I wrote because I was interested in turning this story into my story, because I liked to write, and, for the first time, I wrote because I could take my writing space with me anywhere in the world, whether I was at home or traveling, and I wrote because I wasn't used to having nothing to do with my brain. Just when the text seemed to be finished—I wasn't sure if it really was finished—I unexpectedly got a job as a director's assistant, and I put the text aside for the time being. So the manuscript lay in a drawer for three quiet years. Growing up, I hadn't learned that *life is a competition*, or that it was desirable to be famous, a *star*, as we are now told day in, day out, even by the children's TV shows on every channel, including the public ones, unfortunately. The only thing I'd learned was that life is boring if you're not interested in something. So it was only belatedly, and via various detours, that my manuscript made its way to the Eichborn publishing house, and suddenly they decided that it was already finished as it was, that is, they accepted it and printed it. So the three quiet years that the text had lain there unrecognized hadn't hurt it (or me), they'd helped.

In the course of many theater rehearsals, my teacher Ruth Berghaus taught me not to sidestep, strike through, or set aside the difficulties that suddenly pop up, but rather to acknowledge them and make them into something useful. To work *with* them and not *against* them. Detours are productive. I say that here because I assume that there are some students in the audience who have to work their way forward from *credit point* to *credit point*, as we call them today, in appropriately pseudofinancial terms. Recently a professor of German literature at the University of Vienna told me that she couldn't offer a seminar on Robert Musil's novel *The Man Without Qualities* anymore, because there wasn't enough time for it. It wasn't effective, so to speak, to work through *The Man Without Qualities* in a seminar. So what do the students read in their classes, then? Increasingly they read short stories, she answered. Now, as an author, I have the privilege that most of my books are short, so some students may read them after all.

But still I found her answer shocking, because it seems to me that it's difficult to reach a goal simply by being goal-oriented. It would be nice if the university weren't just something like the gateway to a career, some sort of dues paid to the outside world where you *have* to succeed if you want to pay your rent, if it didn't just give you time to learn how you work, but instead time to learn how you live, to learn what matters to you and what doesn't, if the university could be the affirmation of one's inner life, of a far-off, remote, uncharted, maybe even uncongenial landscape with its own calendar, where those who are seeking their own way have time to get lost, time to take detours, to meet this or that person along the way, to get excited about something, to despair of something, and sometimes just to lie in the grass, look at the clouds passing overhead, and leave room for thoughts to grow. Because what I referred to earlier as the "kernel of truth" may find you where you least expect it.

EARLY MAY 2013

On "The Book Of Words"

BAMBERG LECTURE II

What are my eyes for if they can see but nothing? What are my ears for if they can hear but nothing? Why all this strangeness inside my head?

All of it must be thought into nothingness, one whorl of gray matter at a time, until in the end a spoonful of me will be left glistening at the bottom. I must seize memory like a knife and turn it against itself, stabbing memory with memory. If I can.

Father and mother. Ball. Car. These might be the only words that were still intact when I learned them. Then even they got turned around, ripped out of me and stuck back in upside-down, making the opposite of ball ball, the opposite of father and mother father and mother. What is a car? All the other words had silent halves dragging them down from the start like lead weights around ankles, just as the moon lugs its dark half around with it even when it's full. But it keeps circling in its orbit all the same. For me, words used to be stable, fixed in place, but now I'm letting them all go, if need be I'll cut off a foot if that's the only way to get rid of them. Ball. Ball.

Lullaby and goodnight. *My mother is putting me to bed. She strokes my head as she sings.* White, dry hand stroking the head of a child. With roses bedight. *Eyes the color of water gazing at me; already my eyelids are falling shut.* With lilies o'erspread, *she sings. But lilies are for funerals. Not these lilies, she'd say if she saw the words were making me cry again, they aren't real lilies at all, they're just lilies-of-the-valley for faeries to sleep under. But tonight it's already too late for crying, I've traveled too far into the land of sleep to turn around, and they aren't lilies-of-the-valley, they're real lilies that someone I don't know*

All translations of *Wörterbuch* are quoted from Jenny Erpenbeck, *The Book of Words*, trans. Susan Bernofsky (New York: New Directions, 2007).

is going to lay on my coffin and nail it shut as I sleep. Lay thee down now and rest, *she sings. She pulls the blanket up to my chin and turns out the light. The coffin nails scrape my skin, lots of little bloody wounds.* May thy slumbers be blessed. *And what if they aren't blessed? Then I'll remain lying here in my coffin-bed forever.* May thy slumbers be blessed. *And the drops of blood will turn to stone. Mother.*

Under the military dictatorship in Argentina, from 1976 to 1983, tens of thousands of opponents of the regime *were disappeared*, as the expression went. They were tortured and murdered, only a few of those who were arrested ever returned. These so-called *subversives* included many young people, students, young mothers and fathers, pregnant women. Military officers took the small children of the people they kidnapped, they made the pregnant women give birth in prison hospitals, took the babies, and then killed the mothers. Sometimes they kept the children of the people they murdered, sometimes they sold them to other adherents of the regime. The children's names and birthdates were changed, all documentation of their origins was destroyed.

The period of reckoning immediately after the end of the dictatorship was brief, it only lasted from 1983 to 1986, then came the so-called "Full stop law," and in 1994, an amnesty for the military officers who had temporarily been sentenced to prison.

The "Madres de Plaza de Mayo"—the "Mothers of the Plaza de Mayo"—had already begun their protests in 1977, holding a silent march every week in front of the government building in Buenos Aires to demand information about their disappeared sons and daughters. Even after the fall of the regime, they persisted in their search, and in many cases they managed to find conclusive information about the deaths of their children. But there were some indications that their grandchildren—who had been small children or infants, or hadn't even been born yet their parents were arrested—might have survived. By the mid-1990s, many of these grandchildren were already adults. In about three hundred cases, new methods of genetic testing confirmed the suspicion that a son or daughter was not the biological child of the people he or she had called mother and father for an entire conscious lifetime. In a single moment, the good parents who had raised these children were transformed into liars, and even worse, often into murderers, or at least accessories to or beneficiaries of a murder. The children's own histories were suddenly revealed as a construct. And the *subversives*, who had always been reviled as the enemy by the children's presumptive parents, were suddenly revealed to be their true mothers and fathers, their blood relatives.

Sometime around 2000, I saw a TV report about one of these cases that made an especially strong impression on me: A grown-up daughter learns the truth about her origins, and when her fake father is released in the 1994 amnesty, she's confronted with a choice between him and her biological grandmother, who has finally found her after fifteen years of searching. The daughter refuses to make contact with her grandmother, and decides with full knowledge of the facts to embrace her fake father, the man who murdered her biological parents.

Why, I asked myself, does she choose him, making a choice that goes against the fundamental principles of so many religions, and one that the Catholic church in particular would find evil and wrong? After all, 90 percent of Argentinians are devout Catholics. Thou shalt not kill, as it says in the Ten Commandments. Thou shalt not bear false witness against thy neighbor, it says, thou shalt not lie. And not least: Thou shalt honor thy father and mother. And yet this young woman does not choose her biological grandmother, who lost her own daughter in a crime of state, and who searched for her own granddaughter and finally overcame all obstacles to find her. Instead she chooses a torturer, a murderer, a liar. Given the choice, why did she make the wrong one? Or maybe she didn't really have a choice at all?

How free can we actually be, as individuals, even when we are outwardly, politically free? Whose opinions are they really that we call our own? When can we say *I* and really mean *I*, and not the father, the mother, the teachers, the friends, whose convictions are reproduced in us? How much *I* is there really, beyond my upbringing? (Because even if I reject my upbringing, surely that can be seen as another consequence of my upbringing.) You probably know the famous Schopenhauer quote, it goes something like this: A man can do as he wills, but not will as he wills.

Can we exchange our own history for another? Discard it? Retract it? Can we take the convictions and beliefs that we have developed over the course of years, and replace them with a blank slate? Can we unlearn what we have learned, unfeel what we have felt?

All of those were questions I could not answer. And even if writing is not about answering questions, still some things look different when they're written down, perhaps because writing necessarily condenses things, because it isn't *actually* reality, and so it necessarily has to seek a structure of its own—that is, this condensation must have its own criteria, and suddenly, if you're lucky, this might bring to light what is most essential. You open yourself up to something you don't understand, you put on the life of this or that character like a costume, and then maybe you at least begin to understand, in physical terms, so to speak, why this costume only allows you to move in one way and not in another.

It is an agonizing question, in moral terms, whether a dictatorship that raises the children of the persecuted as its own—rather than killing them together with their parents, as the Nazis did with the children of the Jews—is "better," more humane, or whether it is actually even more evil. However, my intention was not to draw comparisons between the forms of torture and murder practiced in different nations, I didn't want to explicitly set the book in Argentina; instead I wanted to concentrate on asking fundamental questions about the nature and effect of the rituals, extortion mechanisms, and reward strategies that all dictatorships seem to produce—the opposing forces of punishment and praise, the very way that a government offers itself like a father to people who seek the security of childhood, only to exploit these "children" for its own purposes, whatever those purposes might be. This Janus-faced disposition is personified in characters like the father in my book: a split personality who can have an everyday life like other people, have a family like other people, go to work perfectly normally like other people, but that work is torture, deception, or murder. It's astonishing enough, after all, that regardless of what ideology is used to legitimate acts of violence, there are always people to be found, in every country, who will carry out this violence, either with pleasure or at least with dutiful obedience, who will adopt the system's terror as their own calling without even being forced to—at least as long as the system proclaims their innocence.

Surely you have also heard of the famous Milgram experiment, in which a professor instructed his subjects to punish people, supposedly "learners," with electric shocks that gradually increased in intensity over time, ostensibly to help them learn more effectively. The supervisor of the experiment instructed the "perpetrators" to continue even when the "victims" were moaning, screaming in pain, or finally falling silent. Of course there weren't really any electric shocks, and the victims were confederates, their cries of pain were feigned. But the study found that only a third of the subjects in the perpetrator group ultimately decided on their own to stop the torture, in defiance of the supervisor's instructions.

So the monsters aren't always other people, two thirds of us are monsters, too. And of course this has consequences even for those who only share their private lives with these monsters, even *before* the truth is brought to light. For of this I am certain: That which is kept silent takes up just as much space as that which is spoken of openly—and it claims that space, one way or another. But more on that later.

Starting from this concrete case in Argentinian history, my interest was thus drawn to the constitution of experience as such, and within that framework, to the fundamental tactics and possibilities of deception, of silence, the parallel perception of reality.

But there was another reason for me to start the book: One year earlier I had had a child, so I myself was in the process of creating a construct that my son would later call his childhood. Of teaching him the words that would later be his *vocabulary*. I was in the process of experiencing for myself the fact that we never tell children the whole truth at the beginning of their lives, we don't have to, and we can't, because so much of the truth goes beyond a child's capacities of perception, beyond the satisfaction of his needs, and also beyond the scope of his curiosity. So, as a mother, I found myself for the first time tasked with conveying the truth to someone who knew nothing of the world. There's a reason that raising a child is sometimes called a "dictatorship of the parents."

Of course, I could have simply written this young woman's story as it actually happened, with the grandmother's search for her granddaughter, with an initial moment of suspicion, the doubts about her identity, the young woman's ignorance, the genetic analysis, and finally the certainty and all that followed from it. And maybe that wouldn't have been a bad book, maybe it even would have sold better. But I was much more interested in the fact that I could tie myself directly to the story through the medium of my craft, through my words. Because as soon as knowledge and experience are being transmitted, passed on within a given social group, as soon as children are being educated, words become important. Words are abstractions, signs for things that exist in reality—but because words can never actually *be* the things they speak of, because they *must* maintain a certain distance from the things that they describe, it's always possible for something to come between the word and the thing; and so the language that we speak, which can be made up of any possible combination of words, is also susceptible to falsification. *So now can anyone just come*, as it says in my book, *and take a word away from the thing it belongs to . . . , or toss it over some other thing like a blanket, can any person who speaks be a thief? Can he? And what about a person who keeps silent?*

In the book, of course, this has a connection to the child, who is "falsified" herself, but then I also work with words as an author whenever I write. Words grow over the course of a lifetime, but also over the course of a book. They can develop sounds, a rhythm, and they never cease to be something real in themselves: as language and as structure. That means that I can trace the story of my main character's socialization word for word, I can feed the words full of content over the course of the book, so to speak, and in that way I can allow the reader to participate directly in the process by which the truth is suppressed, concealed, and ultimately revealed.

Silence Is Health, for instance, is a motto that I cite in one of the first scenes in the book, a motto that the military had written on a construction fence surrounding a monument in the middle of one of the largest traffic circles in Buenos Aires. *Silent* also describes the snow, a motif that gestures toward the family's Nazi past in Europe, and something that the child, who has never seen snow before, often tries to imagine. *Silence* falls when one of the girl's uncles, who is openly opposed to the regime, repeats over and over at the family dinner table: *And this is quite simply not true.* Later, this uncle will die in a staged car accident. The girl falls *silent* when she is feeding from her wet nurse, her only connection to the normal world outside. The child of Saint Difunta Correa, whose story the girl learns from her wet nurse, is *silenced* in the same way. The miracle in this legend is that the saint's child survives on her mother's breast, even as the mother herself dies of thirst in the desert while trying to make her way with the infant to see her husband, who is imprisoned far away. Two black birds fall *silently* from the sky as the girl watches; later on in the book we learn that they were actually two subversive nuns who were thrown out of a military aircraft. The wet nurse, too, falls *silent*, after someone throws a shoebox over the garden fence, in it she finds the severed hands of her kidnapped daughter: a warning not to say too much to the child entrusted to her care, the girl of my story—after receiving this stark warning, she quits her job, stops talking, falls *silent*. Be *silent*, we say to children. The living are *silent* when there's nothing left to say. When nothing else may be said. And the dead are *silent*. Even though the girl in my book can see and hear the dead, no one else can hear them, no one else can see them. The raucous birthday party that the dead celebrate with the girl is *silent*, nonexistent, for the rest of the family. When the girl finally hears the truth from her father, she too falls *silent*:

Dumb man in the mountain, dumb child on his arm / Dumb the mountain, dumb the child: / Holy dumb man, bless this wound. To staunch the blood.

Be *silent*, don't speak. Don't say what's happening. *Silence is Health.* When the girl, now fully grown, realizes what kind of man her father truly is, she says that her job from now on will be to sleep. Of course, sleeping is also a *silent* matter.

Although a book is usually read silently, and also written silently, *in* writing there is silence and there is sound. There are these blank lines that sometimes leave room to continue breathing, silently, there is the word "silence" with a period after it and then a space.

Silence.

And there is sound:

a drum kit, drum it into him, beating, beating as long as the heart is still beating, when I get home babe, I'm gonna light your fire, gonna wrap my arms around you, hold you close to me, *thwack,* I wanna taste your lips, I wanna kiss you all over, *shards of glass in your cunt, you old sow,* all over, till the night closes in, dance dance dance, it's easy to see when something's right and something wrong, *wham wham wham, thwack, wham wham wham, thwack, instruments made of metal in 4/4 or 3/4 time, it doesn't matter, just so it's louder than he is or she is,* love is thicker than water, *soften him up, him or her, with heat, cold and wet, bring her flesh to the melting point, then we'll see what's at the core, and then crack it between your teeth, crush it, grind it to dust,* stay with me, here with me, near with me, you're my one desire, dance dance dance, I need you babe, shadow dancing, three times a lady, *thwack,* follow me, *you bitch,* thicker than water.

"Beast of Burden" by the Rolling Stones, "Stayin' Alive" by the Bee Gees, "You Don't Bring Me Flowers" by Barbra Streisand and Neil Diamond—these pop songs from 1978 were played at high volume in the torture chambers in the basement of the Marine Academy in Buenos Aires, so that the cries of the tortured couldn't be heard outside. The Rolling Stones, the Bee Gees, and Barbra Streisand had no way of knowing, when they were writing and performing these songs, that their music would be taken away from them like that. Everything that's released into the world follows its own trajectory, and sometimes it returns to us as something foreign, or something that is our own but disfigured, abused.

This book takes up that sort of twofold truth again and again. But how can something like that be integrated into the plot?

Reviews of my works have often claimed that I'm concerned

with childhood, particularly girlhood, but neither *The Old Child* nor *The Book of Words* is actually about a girl. Both books are actually concerned with young women who—for different reasons—critically interrogate their memories, young women who are living in the present, but at the same time in a second present, one that does not want to slip into, does not want to be pushed into, what now goes by the name of the past. Both books required the inclusion of these two perspectives, that of the adult and that of the child, and without these two perspectives I would never have written either book.

To be sure: The child's-eye view provides us—as readers who know more than the child knows, or who at least learn more in the course of our reading—with necessary insights. The child's-eye view *can* only begin to take shape on the basis of the words that are spoken to the child, and the child's-eye view *must* always assume the best, if the child is to learn to live. And so it renders these cruel realities—the absurd physical barbarities that take place in the torture chambers, the presumptive father's wicked psychological manipulation of the child—more clearly and more painfully than any adult opinion founded on this or that moral framework ever could. But the child's perspective can only have this effect when it is considered in comparison to all that the child was never told, that is, when the perspective itself can be seen. In other words: when the child's perspective has already been lost.

As an author, you sometimes wish that the critics would look a bit more closely—I say that just in case there are any future critics sitting in the audience ...

Here is an example of one moment in the book when these two worlds collide, as if by accident:

When fish is served, everyone is given a special knife that isn't sharp. But when we are eating meat, I have to use my child's knife, the handle of which has a cat's face engraved in it. Then my mother cuts my meat into little pieces with her knife, which is pointed and jagged-edged, and my knife with the cat is only for pushing the bits she's cut onto my fork. The handle of my fork has a bear on it, and the spoon has a rabbit. If a knife is sharp enough, you can cut all the way around the soles of a man's or even a woman's feet and then peel back the skin. After all, this man or this woman will no longer have far to walk to reach the land of the dead. And some word is always the last one. Knife perhaps. Or some other one. Some word this man or this woman has always known.

The old truth and the new truth collide like this again and again in *The Book of Words*, the things that the girl learned and experienced as a child are there, but they lack an organic connection to the things that she learns and experiences as an adult. There is no continuity, no development, from one to the other. The growth is cut away. And the tension that this creates can't be resolved. There is a passage in the book that relates to this very question, if only indirectly:

A bird was walking here, my father says. Squatting down beside me, he points out the star-shaped scratches in the dark soil at the edge of our garden, in the shade of the trees where no grass grows. . . . What is a track, I ask my father. A trace that is left behind, something that cannot be caused by chance, my father replies. . . . But then before you can know what cannot be caused by chance, I say, you have to know everything else. Probably, my father says. And what about the double time a track like this has. What double time, my father says. The time, I say, when the bird was walking here, and then the second time, when we see it was here—the track is a sort of bridge between them. Perhaps, my father says. But by the time you're finally old enough to tell the difference between chance and everything else, you're too heavy to walk across the bridge. No, my father says, that's silly, and he picks up a little stick and starts making star-shaped scratches beside the star-shaped scratches.

There are moments in every life when a second truth becomes manifest: when someone you love has cheated on you; when everyone else at work knows that you're about to get fired, but you don't find out yourself until the last day; when a sickness that you've been carrying around for a long time without knowing it suddenly becomes acute, etc. There are many ways to lose what we generally refer to as innocence. But all of these discoveries have one thing in common: We suddenly begin to read the past differently. The same building blocks that were always there now come together to constitute a different reality. Events that simply happened before suddenly become legible as signs. There's a line from Goethe that's always useful to recall in this context: *We only see what we know*. It's often painful to learn a new way of reading things after they have gotten so jumbled up, we often wish that we could retreat to that state of blindness, into the idyllic world we knew before, as if that were a form of recovery; but without these painful discoveries, how could we find the right tools for the real existing world—if we even could? What remains in each case is the consciousness that there may always be other truths beyond those that are readily apparent, a certain relativization of our own horizons. For some, this experience may ripen into a chronic mistrust, but for others it may lead through skepticism to the point where an egocentric world-view is upended.

Earlier I said that the tension between one truth and another can't be resolved, I'd like to expand on that now: One wonderful aspect of literature is that merely by naming this unresolvable tension, it casts a sort of spell, and while it may not give us the one, irrefutable truth, it does provide us with a structure that allows us to observe the many truths that exist parallel to one another, to consider them precisely *in parallel*. Language can achieve the paradox of capturing a whole wide world in just a few concrete words, and when this experiment is successful, then it may also achieve the reverse, transforming the rigid individual criteria according to which *one* man assesses what happens to *him* into something living and open, something connected to the whole world. Literature is indiscreet, its purpose is to be intimate, to tear secrets wide open—not for the sake of selling more books, but rather to allow us, the readers, to see and to perceive as much as possible, to perceive more than one person alone normally can. But literature can also accomplish other things by these same means. For instance, it can break open the secret places where people are tortured, reintroducing them into the world that we are ordinarily aware of, it can carry the disappearance of subversives *ad absurdum*, and in this sense it can offer solidarity, at least in spirit, to counteract the isolation of these prisoners, the lostness of people like those in my book who were tortured in the basements beneath the shopping center in Buenos Aires as loud pop music played. It does away with the division of the world into two parts: the one familiar, the other kept silent. We see the stores where people shop, and beneath the floors of those shops we see the basement where at that very moment people are being tortured; we see the soccer field, but we also see the people buried beneath the grass; we see a delivery truck painted with a fish and the slogan *Fresh Products*, but we also see the political prisoner who is being transported in that truck, which no one is supposed to know about. Literature tells us that what we know is never the whole truth, but literature also tells us that the whole truth is waiting for us, if only we could read. And with that, it begins to teach us to read, even if that lesson requires more time to learn than we have in our own lifetimes.

It also teaches us—and here I include myself as a writer—that the truth never ends where we want it to end. In my book, the father is clearly evil, the daughter is clearly an innocent child, her true parents are clearly the victims. But we also have to ask ourselves at what cost the murdered parents stood up for what is right. We have to recognize that someone who tortures people from 8 a.m. to 4 p.m. can still be a loving father at home. We can't close our eyes to the fact that love can also take an unformed child and shape that child, at a certain point, into someone who crosses over to the other side, someone who begins to take the side of hate, despite knowing better. The woman at the center of my book is so interesting because she ransoms her life with her own life. In order to protect herself, she gives up her own origins. She can't win either way, no matter what decision she makes. And yet she has to make a decision. Doesn't she? When we read—and when we write, too—we have to live with the fact that the world can't be divided into good and evil, into wins and losses, that the truth is made up of many layers, that most things can be read from both sides, that some questions can't be answered. We have to live with the fact that certain questions are met with silence. And that is sometimes truly difficult.

No doubt we would like it to be simpler: We would like to know that when we give something, we get something in return, because we've learned over the course of millions of years that mutual aid is necessary to our survival, and we've also learned to exploit each other to survive. In other words, we're used to believing that our actions have consequences, and that we can roughly anticipate those consequences at the moment of action, otherwise we wouldn't be able to act in this world. But the true scope of the consequences that our actions will have for other people and other creatures—whether in the long run or even in that moment—is greater than we can comprehend at first (or possibly ever). Surely that's a good thing, since otherwise we'd probably lose the ability to act altogether, to decide anything whatsoever. Of course we can't know (and don't want to know) that our actions may have to be taken back at some point, either by us or by others, that they will have to be revised or undone, that they reveal something about us and not just about themselves. We see our own actions as the beginning of a chain of events, but they may actually be the end, or the middle, of a long series of actions performed by other people or other creatures we've never heard of.

Recently, at a literary event, I met someone who said that he knew me much better than I knew him—not from Wikipedia, but because he'd shared a train compartment with me while I told a friend all sorts of things about my family and my everyday life. So I was someone for him, I was a person he remembered, while he wasn't someone I would have remembered. Things like that, it often strikes me, are happening all the time.

And then I often think of the Grimms' fairy tales, like the one about Mother Holle. A widow has a beautiful, hard-working stepdaughter, Gold Mary, and an ugly, lazy daughter, Pitch Mary. First Gold Mary falls down the well, and she unexpectedly comes out in the land of Mother Holle, but she doesn't know that there's a reward in store for her when she hears baked bread crying for help and takes it out of the oven, when she gathers apples, or when she makes Mother Holle's bed, giving it a thorough shake each time. She moves through the world without knowing that everything she does is a test. And maybe it's not even meant as a test, maybe it's just a way of acting in the world, one which Mother Holle later values and rewards. Pitch Mary, on the other hand, already knows that it's a test, and expects to be rewarded, but she doesn't do the right thing, so she misses her chance. So knowledge alone is not enough.

But what is enough, then?

Why does the stepdaughter do the right thing, but not the daughter?

Why does God accept the sacrifice of Abel, the shepherd, but not the sacrifice of Cain, the farmer?

The story of Cain and Abel could be meant to represent the

transition from the nomadic shepherd to the sedentary farmer. But it could also be meant to demonstrate God's capriciousness, his omnipotence, to teach the faithful a sense of humility in the face of that omnipotence. On the other hand, it could also be meant to demonstrate that evil obeys its own law. So, is it the omnipotence and capriciousness of evil? A comparison of God and the devil? Or is it a matter of teaching honesty, of putting someone who has done wrong to the test? Would God have forgiven Cain if Cain had confessed to his deed? Does evil always entail denial? But that would mean that the evil man is always at least acting within the same system of values as the good man. Is there hope then? And doesn't God forgive Cain when he places the mark upon him? That mark is not a sign that Cain is cast out, as is often believed, but rather a sign that—although and precisely because he has been cast out—Cain enjoys the protection of God. *Whosoever slayeth Cain, vengeance shall be taken on him sevenfold*. Another question that is no less interesting: Why is the Judeo-Christian family tree so decisively shaped by God's capriciousness and by Cain's murder of his brother, since the good son Abel is the one who is killed … So there are thousands of layers that come together to produce something like truth, and the world is surely always much larger than it appears at first, or second, or even third glance.

Years ago, I cut an article out of *Der Spiegel*, and it's been hanging on my refrigerator ever since. The author writes:

> In order to learn about the human sense of justice, anthropologists played the so-called Ultimatum Game with members of 15 primitive tribes: The first player receives a certain amount of money and can decide how much he gives to the second player. The second player has to decide whether or not to accept the offer. If he refuses, neither of the players gets the money.
>
> In industrialized countries, the offer is usually half of the total

amount. An even split is generally considered acceptable. But if the first player only offers a quarter (e.g. 25 euros out of 100), the second player generally refuses—knowing full well that he will also go home empty-handed.

The results among the primitive tribes varied dramatically. For instance, the Machiguenga in the Peruvian rainforest frequently offered only 20 percent, which the second player would gladly accept. That was consistent with their way of life: Family members generally stick together and share very little with outsiders. In those circumstances, the second player can be happy to get anything at all.

The Gnau people of Papua New Guinea saw things very differently. They offered up to 70 percent—which the second player frequently refused. In the Gnau culture, social status depends to a great extent on how much one gives to others. Those who tried to score points with especially high offers appeared pretentious. What's more, in some cases the second players presumably feared that they would be expected to reciprocate at some point in the future. It would be better not to accept the gift at all.

Of course, predictability has a great deal to do with questions of truth and lies, with possibilities of control and planning, but it also has to do with possibilities of trade and the maximization of profit that play a decisive role in our world. In another article in *Der Spiegel*, about an enormous shopping mall in China that has been standing empty ever since it was completed in 2005, we read: *The larger China's building projects become, the more often the country's government and entrepreneurs seem to run up against the limits of predictability. It turns out that the people, who were seen for two generations as the pliable masses required to carry out five-year plans, aren't actually predictable in the end. China's state capitalists still refuse to accept this insight.*

However, "this insight" itself comes from a world in which the predictability of human action is at the very center of economic thought, a world in which research into the souls of potential customers is precisely what makes it possible to calculate future profits. There it is again: this freedom and the other freedom. Certainly it doesn't hurt to have grown up in a system where we learned not to trust what we read in the newspapers. In the context of this excursus about surveillance societies, allow me to share with you a few wonderful sentences by Alexander Kluge that are also hanging on my refrigerator door:

> *It is a matter of observation that there are limits to what people will put up with. At unexpected points that cannot be determined in advance, people develop a will of their own. No disappointment can fully exhaust the reserve of hope. What we can do is devote boundless effort to the concrete areas in which we ourselves work. Whether that will prove useful in the end is, to put it melodramatically, in God's hands; but you could also say that it's in all of our hands. Human willfulness is reliable and invincible. It returns again and again. It is a phoenix.*

Let us hope so, for the Chinese, and also for ourselves.

In closing, I would like to return to a central motif of the book, the motif of silence, of concealment. A few years ago, I wrote a short story with a similar theme that features just this sort of silence:

> *Quite a few people who live in the neighborhood know that her mother wasn't pregnant back then, but the daughter herself doesn't know. The woman went and fetched herself the child overnight. When the daughter goes out, many eyes rest on her with the same thought: Her mother was never pregnant. The daughter walks through a forest of stares, an endless forest, but she doesn't know that this forest is what makes everything around her so dark.*

There are many things in life, of course, that can be thought but not spoken, and they aren't all so serious. When I was taking a three-week acting class as part of my theater degree, our teacher gave us the assignment to stand up two at a time, facing each other. When he gave the signal, we were supposed to tell each other everything we were thinking about our partners at that moment. We quickly realized what that would mean, and we refused to do the exercise. Our justification: We had no intention of becoming actors, the closest any of us would come was dramaturgy—so radical openness wasn't something that we needed to learn and endure for the sake of our careers, and this two-minute exercise would make it impossible for us to keep studying together. *Man can face the truth*, as the fine and famous line by Ingeborg Bachmann puts it. But there is *one* kind of person who is probably least prepared of all to accept the truth: the person who conceals it. To conceal something is not just to keep it quiet; to conceal something can also mean to knowingly give the wrong answer to a question from time to time, to equivocate, to deflect, it can also mean to think for an extra moment before responding or reacting to someone else's observation, long enough to commit so firmly to an alternate reality that it seems believable. Surely there are also good, well-intentioned, even honorable reasons to conceal something, but whenever something is concealed, there is always something there, never nothing. And the question that always arises is whether this concealment achieves its aim—be it happiness, security, family harmony, or simply calm. Because whatever is concealed doesn't disappear, it remains and continues its existence, follows its own paths, sometimes it even turns up unexpectedly, intruding again into the life in which it was concealed. But as long as the concealer maintains his alternate reality, his parallel world, he can never meet the person from whom he conceals the truth on an equal footing, so concealment also tells us something about a loneliness that touches both sides.

In my play *Cats Have Nine Lives*, there is a line: *People have the freedom to say whatever they want to say*. Of course, that can only be true if a person who lies or conceals has made his own rules for living together with others, has chosen not to recognize the rules that others accept, and has also neglected to inform others of his choice. It may be that the father in *The Book of Words* only *fully* "buys" his stolen daughter at the moment when he first tells her about his own rules, his own world, while they are on the run together. He knows that it makes a difference whether *he* is the one who tells his daughter about these things—and tells her about them with unsparing, unbearable openness—or whether she only learns what he has done and what he has concealed from her when he appears in court. Only through *his* disclosure can she become his accomplice, only if he, the father she loves, tears down the barrier that he has always maintained between them, thus initiating her into his *whole* world. We can shut ourselves off from others, but not from ourselves.

So disclosure is likewise a precarious act, disclosure, too, can be an instrument of power. Whatever we have learned stays with us. Sometimes when I read a poem by Goethe or Hölderlin, I am jealous of the worlds that Goethe and Hölderlin knew, where they didn't have to know what an assembly point was, or a gas wagon, or Zyklon B. But for us, today, as we go for a walk, eat, drink, write, have conversations, dig up a flower bed, go shopping, take a child by the hand, lie in the sun, listen to music, we have to know the whole time where the enormous piles of eyeglasses or shoes came from, the ones we see in the black-and-white photographs that we encounter every so often, we have to know what *selection* meant at a certain point in time, to know that experiments were conducted in the use of human bones to produce soap. We always know it. Fundamentally. And since we know it, we cannot simply live, we must live *past* this knowledge—it doesn't stop us from going for a walk, eating, drinking, and so on. And yet, because of what happened—and because we know what happened—everything that we do is completely transformed, even if it has not changed at all.

At the end of my book, the young woman learns something that she would never have wanted to learn. We learn it too. Does it help to look these things in the face—the monstrous things that really happened, and that are still happening today, maybe not in Europe, but elsewhere in the world? Does it help to disclose these horrible things, so that *nothing like that*, as it's always said, *can ever happen again*? To be honest, I don't know. I don't know if experience can be transmitted by oral or written storytelling. Knowledge, yes, information, yes, but experiences may be something that every generation has to discover anew for itself. And yet there is one thing that may be possible—it may be possible to do away with the secrecy that allows terror to be transformed into a deadly weapon. The weight that we carry, as people who know of these terrors, is one that we take from the shoulders of those who were selected to disappear from the face of the earth for one reason or another, and who are still being selected, perhaps for other reasons, in other cities and countries.

I once heard that Schiller's furniture was stored in the Buchenwald concentration camp for a while during the Second World War. In Schiller's day, the German princes earned money by rounding up young men in their own lands by force and selling them to England, the English then sent these men to fight in the American Revolutionary War, and only a few survived. If any of the young men refused, they were killed on German soil. Can horror be compared to horror, violence to violence, death to death? Certainly not. And yet. In closing, let us hear two lines from Schiller, who did not have to know when he wrote them where his furniture would one day be stored:

> *Even to be a lament in the mouth of the loved one is glorious,*
> *For what is common sinks in silence to the Kingdom of the Dead.* *

LATE MAY 2013

---

* Translated in Michael Steinberg, *Choral Masterworks: A Listener's Guide* (New York: Oxford University Press, 2005), 83.

Speech and Silence

The difference between speech and silence.
> Speaking at all.
> And why.
> What can be named, but isn't there.
> What is there, but cannot be named.

"The Hour We Knew Nothing of Each Other" is a play by Peter Handke in which not a single word is spoken—a magnificent idea. He writes, for example:

A woman with a scarf around her head and rubber boots crosses the square lugging a watering can and also carrying a bunch of wilting, no, already rotting flowers which she throws off stage in a high arc.

Right after her an almost identically dressed woman comes in from a completely different place, type: old hag, with a sickle, a bunch of evergreens and a basket filled to the brim with wild mushrooms. *

And so on.

In my first book, *The Old Child*, which I've already spoken of here once, there is hardly any direct dialogue. There is this:
When the teacher says . . . , the girl answers him.

In the second book, *The Book of Words*, which I spoke about two weeks ago on this spot, there are ghosts who speak to the main character, and there is the father, the mother, the friend.

But all of the dialogue in both books is filtered through time,

---

* Peter Handke, "The Hour We Knew Nothing of Each Other," trans. Gitta Honegger, *Theater* 24, no. 1 (February 1, 1993): 96.

so to speak, through a second layer of consciousness with which this or that main character remembers the dialogues or puts them to the test, looks at them as something unfamiliar, as part of a successful performance, or calls them back to mind to examine them for traces of something that she didn't know back when those dialogues were taking place, when they were in the present.

For instance, when we encounter the "old child," she is searching for a language she can speak that will allow her to fit in with fourteen-year-olds.

The girl is in search of something, she is trying to speak, but while the vocabulary itself appears to have nothing wrong with it, there is always a black, gaping nothingness that can be glimpsed through it, as through filigree. Everything that comes out of her mouth always looks like a lie, even if it isn't one. . . . The girl's sentences lie in her stomach like a heap of scrap metal, they cannot take root inside her, and sometimes she even looks down to see whether one of these sentences isn't poking out of her side.

In *The Book of Words*, too, there is a great deal of mistrust with respect to language and its capriciousness, which stems from the fact that some things are disclosed while others are not, a mistrust apparent even in the book's title. In the course of her search for the stories that have *created* her identity, the main character is driven to ask questions: Where do words—and with them, language and thought—come from, and what effect do they have?

The man in the pulpit is telling the story of Creation, and if I understand correctly, what happened was that reality filled God's words to the brim with all the things God spoke of when he still had no one to talk to but himself: The trees grew into his word tree, the fish swam after his word fish and quickly slipped into it between scales that were already there from his speaking of scales, the birds darted up to the sky, following the feath-

*ers God had already proclaimed, and pulled them on over their heads, and Adam and Eve filled the words Adam and Eve with blood, bones, kidneys, intestines, heart, eyes and mouth and all the rest of what God talked about to himself when he was still alone. . . . Why does mankind have so many different languages? I ask my father as we are walking back to his parents' house hand in hand after the service. So now can anyone just come and take a word away from the thing it belongs to, I ask, or toss it over some other thing like a blanket, can any person who speaks be a thief? . . . God must have been terribly lonely before he began with Creation, otherwise a person doesn't speak to himself of kidneys and bones.**

For the "old child," as for the young woman in *The Book of Words*, the language that people use to understand one another is no longer something that can simply be understood, it is no longer self-evident. And this reflection *about* something that was once said, or about something that is being said right now, can take the form of prose: why this or that person probably says (or does) this or that, how it is said, in what way, or what consequences follow from it, what conclusions this or that person draws from what is said, what this or that person leaves unsaid and why, or what he or she imagines while something very different is said, whether by him- or herself or by others, the digressions, the possible meanings and interpretations of what is said—when I write prose, I can write about all of that.

I remember being very hesitant to use dialogue to advance the plot of *The Old Child*. It seemed wrong to me to have my character reveal herself in that way. That's partly because this particular girl is an especially closed-off character, but also because a sentence that is spoken is always a sentence that is spoken—"there's no two ways about it," as my mother used to say. In a dialogue

* All translations of *Wörterbuch* are quoted from Jenny Erpenbeck, *The Book of Words*, trans. Susan Bernofsky (New York: New Directions, 2007).

we are in the present and only in the present. We see the person who is speaking before us in the flesh, with his manner of speaking, with his vocabulary, with his manipulation of words, perhaps with his employment of a particular language, and we not only observe *with* him, but also, and above all, we observe *the person himself* as he speaks, as he remains silent, or as he tries to hide behind the words that he speaks. Yes, we *also* see a world through his eyes, but above all we see the person himself: naked, as a part of the world. When we know nothing about a character except what he himself says—nothing that can put those things in perspective—then we are no longer behind the lines, we are on the front.

It was not so much fear as reverence that I felt as I told the artistic director of the theater in Graz that I would try to write a play for two women over the summer—he had given me the assignment to direct a production, but I hadn't been able to find an appropriate play for the cast. So suddenly I found myself in the situation of not only experimenting with dialogue, but being forced to write *only* dialogue, since without dialogue there's no play (with the one exception of the Peter Handke play I've already mentioned).

B sits on the only chair. A appears, B rises, A sits down. During the following scenes the teacher continually corrects the posture of the student.

A: The chair is warm.

B: Sorry.

A: I don't like it when my chair is warm from other people.

B: Okay.

A: Okay! If you really want to study with me, then take note of two things immediately.

B: I'm not allowed to sit on your chair.

A: Three things.

B: What?

A: You have to know your place.

B: Okay.

A: That's the second thing.

B: What?

A: Your speech. You must keep in mind at all times that your speech is your dress. When the dress is dirty, no one will buy anything from you. But selling is how we earn our living.

B: Okay.

A: *Is silent.*

B: Sorry. But I can explain about the chair. I thought—

A: The third thing is that you should stop making unfounded assumptions. Do you think anyone is interested in what you think?

B: Fine then.

A: Fine then is not an answer.

B: No.

A: Good. So get used to observing, holding your tongue, and when you open your mouth, don't lose track of what you're saying.

B: Okay. Good. Yes.*

Heiner Müller once wrote: *The words / fall irretrievably into the clockwork of time / making things recognizable or unrecognizable. / What is deadly to man is what is unrecognizable.* These magnificent sentences often go through my head.

So I wrote as if my dialogues had to bear witness to what goes wrong when people try to understand each other. I wrote dialogues in which the speakers are hardheaded or disagreeable, in which they refuse to express themselves in their speech, or only

---

* All translations from *Katzen haben sieben Leben* are quoted from Jenny Erpenbeck, "Cats Have Nine Lives," trans. Di Brandt, *PAJ: A Journal of Performance and Art* 41, no. 1 (January 1, 2019): 95–128. The translation has been amended slightly to match the German edition of the published lecture.

speak in order to provoke, to educate, to conceal themselves, perhaps also to seduce or harm one another—in order to do anything possible *except* what could lead to a real encounter between their two inner worlds. Indeed, whenever people speak, it fundamentally raises the question of whether words can ever lead to understanding. It was the unresolved and the unresolvable that interested me.

Precisely by placing very ordinary dialogues in the spotlight, dialogues that any one of us might become involved in at some point in our lives, I could make the mute language *behind* the dialogue audible. Whatever is written is put on display. And whatever is put on display ceases to be self-evident. Or better: it *shows* itself to be something that was never self-evident to begin with.

In writing dialogues, I inevitably found myself constantly confronted with characters as they exist within the context of relationships—not as "lone wolves."

Words and speech in a play are an instrument, I saw, they are *more* of an instrument than the narrative language of a story or a novel—or at least they are an instrument of a different kind. When I write prose, it remains *my* instrument, the author's instrument, whereas in a play it is the instrument with which the figures lash out at one another. As I said, I was in the middle of a battle: None of the characters could hide behind the protective shield of my prose to "think things over in peace," and I couldn't hide behind the protective shield of my characters, it was no longer a question of what world I created for them, rather the only question that mattered was what each of them revealed about himself to whatever world it was that he lived in, to his world—and what he did not reveal. A sentence that is spoken is a confession, no matter what meanings may be layered beneath it, no matter what it means in truth, no matter what it leaves unsaid; we perceive the sentence as the very flesh of the character.

The words of a play fly past our ears like stones, and the person who throws these stones doesn't explain why, but we see him as he raises his arm. We see him as he hurls the stones. He doesn't see himself, he is only concerned with his own survival. He doesn't want to deceive his author, at most he wants to deceive his opponent, and he doesn't want to explain his combat tactics to us, the audience, or to tell us the reasons for his rage. Everything that we want to see can only be seen in the way that he aims, in the way that he hits or misses the target, in the power or the weakness of his throw, in his hesitation, in the way that he takes cover, perhaps in the way that he flees, in his feints, his ambushes, and perhaps in the way that he wins or loses. In him, himself. In him alone. And also, of course, in the person who is his target, his antagonist. But he is no longer talking to *us*.

As an author of prose, I had always looked *with* the character, but now I had to set the character loose, the character had better things to do than talk to me. What made me the author wasn't the text itself, the content of the text, but only the fact that I wrote down the dialogue. Because by writing down the dialogue, I very clearly set myself apart from it. I defended myself against it—a proxy for all those who are rendered silent by this dialogue or similar ones. Who are caught, devoured, by dialogues like this. Those who do *not* succeed in keeping their distance.

But why is a good play so interesting, anyway? Because it is filled with surprises and transformations. Because every sentence that is spoken, or left unspoken, allows a situation to be read in a new way. Because a conversation is always an extremely complex interplay of action and reaction. An answer is an answer to something that preceded it, but it is also a thing of its own, its own beginning, which demands another reaction. Of course, there can be a lifetime full of similar sentences, and only at the age of 50 does the character grab an ax and murder someone—or, instead, he goes out to the yard and takes a deep breath. And yet each one of those similar sentences over the course of those 50 years contributes in some way to the fact that the character eventually picks up that ax—or goes out to the yard and takes a deep breath. The transformation of a quantity into a new quality is always a movement, though sometimes a very slow one. And movement is always interesting—even, sometimes especially, when it is very slow.

But what keeps this movement going? That's what we call the *action*. There are twelve *actions*, or plots, of this sort in my play *Cats Have Nine Lives*. Two women act twelve times, they interact twelve times, they win or they lose, but of course the currency in question isn't money, rather it's love or hate or success or power or submission. The women act, that is to say: From scene to scene, over the course of the twelve transformations of the two main characters, they carry along with them an imbalance, and this imbalance is the source of the failures, the teetering, the death, and the violence. This imbalance is the engine that drives the play—the perpetuum mobile—it is the engine that makes *action* necessary, and that's why it doesn't come to rest until the very end: at the moment when, for the first time, one of the characters sacrifices something for the other without duress—exhibiting generosity.

This is just what it means to write a play, or to read a play or see one in the theater: to observe through the dialogue how the power relations begin to teeter, how they are reversed, and then perhaps reversed again, or maybe not? In a very short span of time, we can observe how an intention gives rise to something, how this something matures and then becomes a thing of its own with a will of its own. In other words, how relationships are constantly in motion, how relationships themselves are like an organic being. This can go well, or it can go badly. It can go well at first and then go badly. And then go well again. And then go badly again in the end. Every play, by its very nature, is full of time bombs. Here's another example from my *Cats* play:

B is a baby. A, the mother, holds it in her arms.

B: *Screams.*

A: Stop screaming, I tell you.
   Shakes B.

B: *Screams.*

A: Want to know what Mommy's going to do now, you little piece of shit?
   Throws B down and picks up a rope.

B: *Stops screaming.*

A: Mommy's going outside now to hang herself with this rope.

B: *Holds onto the mother and starts screaming again.*

A: *Starts screaming and howling herself.*
   Because you're unbearable, because you're an unbearable little screaming turd.
   Shakes the child off and leaves the house with the rope.

Time passes.

B as an adolescent locks all the doors, takes the key, sits down, and waits with the key in her lap, staring at the window. A comes home.

A: Tell me, what kind of game is this?

B: I was scared.

A: Are you trying to cause terror here, young lady?

B: No.

A: Who do you think you are?

B: Nobody.

A: Fine then. Did you wash the dishes?

B: No.

A: Did you vacuum?

B: No.

A: Do you think I'm your maid?

B: I couldn't.

A: What does that mean, I couldn't.

B: I was scared.

A: The young lady was scared.
   Do you know how sick I am of this?

B: *Shakes her head.*

A: I've had it up to here, up to here.

B: *Nods.*

A: Do you know what Mommy's going to do now?

B: *Shakes her head.*

A: Mommy's going out now to hang herself with this rope.
   A leaves the room with the rope in her hand.

Time passes.

B is pregnant.

A: You're pregnant?

B: *Nods.*

A: That can't be true.

B: *Is silent.*

A: A child with a child. That just can't be true.

B: *Is silent.*

A: There's no father, I suppose.

B: *Shakes her head.*

A: Well, if you think I'll take care of your brat just because you're too dumb to be careful when you're fucking, you're fooling yourself.

B: *Is silent.*

B loses the child.

Time passes.

A lies in bed.

A: It's too bright.

B pulls the curtains around the bed so that A is hidden. B stands before the curtained bed, from which the voice of A can be heard.

A: Did you wash the dishes?

B: Yes.

A: Did you vacuum?

B: Yes.

A: So shitty that I have to lie here.
   You pushed me.

B: But that's not true. I wasn't even there.

A: To push your own mother.

B: I told you to wait in front of the store, but you ran off.

A: You left me alone on purpose. You were waiting to see me fall.

B: That's not true. I was shopping, and only wanted you to wait outside and rest.

A: Yes, yes, okay. Got your wish, didn't you? So now I'm lying here.

B: But Mommy.

A: You're probably angry that I'm not dead.

B: Stop.

A: You see, now everything is turned around.
   I busted my ass my whole life for you and now see how it is.
   Now you can do what you want with me.

B: But I don't want to do anything with you.

A: Well, think about it. You can poison me if you want.

B: I don't want to poison you.

A: I could see it in you, how much you hate me.

B: I don't hate you, Mommy.

A: Ah, then you must pity me.

B: Yes, I pity you.

A: You're thinking, ah, the old cripple.

B: You'll be able to walk again, you're not a cripple.

A: Of course I'm a cripple. At last you've got your way. Now you can do what you want with me.

B: Ah, Mommy.

Time passes.

A is carried out of the room on a covered stretcher. B takes the rope and hangs herself.

What happens? At the beginning we have a mother who clearly has weak nerves, and a child who is terrorizing the mother with her screams. The mother seems weak. Doesn't she?

Later on, the mother begins to coerce the child using psychological torture—making use of her own evident weakness, a means of coercion that is known to be very effective. The child seems weak. Doesn't she?

Then—the mother has become an old woman in a wheelchair, she's clearly suffering from her dependence on her daughter, the daughter remains unwaveringly calm and composed in the face of her mother's attempts to provoke her. The daughter seems strong. Doesn't she?

The mother dies. The daughter hangs herself, carrying out her mother's threats against her own body.

We recall Schopenhauer's words that I have already cited once from this podium: *A man can do as he wills, but not will as he wills.* Is the daughter strong or weak in the end? Is her suicide an escape, or unconscious obedience to the mother's orders, or the fulfillment of something that the mother never dared to do? The possible answers to these questions are left open—and in this unresolved cadence, so to speak, the whole complexity of the mother-daughter relationship is contained: all of the growth, all of the vulnerability, all of the uncertainties and silences, all of the surrenders, all of the hopes.

What does that mean in concrete terms? It means: A play is unthinkable without everything that is *not* spoken of, everything that *cannot* be said. Silence is essential, it is the inseparable shadow of what is spoken. Only through this negative image can the words that are spoken tell us anything at all. Only when those words extend beyond themselves, into the silence. Where the text not only *has* content, but *is* content itself.

Plays displace the weight of reflection and empathy onto the reader / spectator by deciding what the characters reveal in their speech—whether the characters within the play consciously manipulate what is revealed, or whether this decision is made completely unconsciously. The characters within the play cannot escape the fact that they are being observed. And the further their own revelations diverge from the play's actual center of gravity, its fulcrum, the less those characters manage to escape what I will refer to here as the play's "moral lever." Thus the energy contained in every good play is mostly communicated indirectly, even in those scenes where one actor or another seems to express himself very clearly: screaming or crying, pulling out all the hairs on his head one at a time, collapsing and dying. Tragedy is fundamentally something that always takes place behind the words, behind what can be spoken and acted out, and indeed, the cause of the tragedy often lies precisely in this impossibility: in the fact that the words required to reach an understanding are lacking, that they are not forthcoming, they are refused, or they may not be spoken. So precisely at the moments when the words express something very different from the heart of the matter, something is set in motion, an inner movement occurs within the reader or spectator. When I say movement, I am not only speaking of being moved in emotional terms, but also of a movement that occurs in our thoughts.

That is to say, there is always silence in good texts, it is a synonym for the essential thing that remains unspeakable; but in technical terms, this silence takes two forms:

First, silence may be a sort of primer coat, a foundation, while, on a superficial level, people carry on speaking, chattering, often more than ever.

Second, of course, there are points where real silence falls.

I would like to read you an example of the first kind of silence, the silence that accompanies a loquacious passage, that adds its own commentary—in this case it is the silence not of the speaker, but rather of one of the others present in this "scene." The passage comes from Thomas Bernhard, and in order to create utter confusion, I will read a passage from a work of prose—his novel *Woodcutters*. The situation is as follows: The narrator is invited to a so-called *artistic dinner*, and he observes what takes place there. The guests have been awaiting the arrival of an actor from the Burgtheater who is playing the role of Ekdal in Ibsen's *The Wild Duck*, and now that he has finally arrived at 12:30 a.m. following a performance, they can begin their dinner:

Ekdal, he said, spooning up his soup, has been my dream role *for decades. And then he went on, interrupting himself after every other word to spoon up more soup,* Ekdal—*pause for a spoonful*—has always—*another spoonful*—been my—*another spoonful*—favorite part, *adding, after two more spoonfuls,* for decades. *And the phrase* dream role *he actually pronounced as though it denoted some culinary delicacy.* Ekdal is my favorite role, *he said several times, and I immediately wondered whether he would have said that Ekdal was his favorite role had he had no success in it. When an actor is successful in a certain role he says it's his*

*favorite: when he isn't, he doesn't, I thought. The actor went on spoon-
ing up his soup and repeating that Ekdal was his favorite role. For a long
time none of the other guests said anything, but merely ate their soup and
stared at the actor, as though he were the only one entitled to speak. When
he ate fast, they ate fast; when he slowed down, they slowed down; and
by the time he had finished the last spoonful, so had they. Long after they
had finished their soup I still had half a plateful left. I did not like the
taste, and so I did not eat it.* **

I was not surprised to learn that Thomas Bernhard actually
wanted to be a singer. Because even though the passage that I've
just read is prose, it's very clear that the content is strongly ex-
pressed through the music of the language, through the rhythm,
through the practically manic use of the same sounds over and
over, through this insistence, on a level beyond content, that
emerges in the mechanical depiction of the speech and the dinner, which ultimately proves to be the inverse of that most essential thing, the silent, deeply skeptical act of observation.

The other silence that I mentioned before is, as I said, ex-
pressed in the actual absence of words, in the quiet that ensues.
At the end of Goethe's *Iphigenia in Tauris,* there is one of the
most wonderful examples of this sort of presence of the essential, unspeakable thing in a moment of silence, when Iphigenia
asks her host and friend Thoas to bid her farewell, after he has
learned that he will have to surrender her, the woman he loves,
forever, because her brother Orestes wants to take her with him.

Then, go! says Thoas.

And Iphigenia answers him:

* Thomas Bernhard, *Woodcutters,* trans. David McLintock (New York: Vintage International, 2010), 101.

Not so, my king! I cannot part
Without thy blessing, or in anger from thee:
Banish us not! the sacred right of guests
Still let us claim: so not eternally
Shall we be severed. Honored and beloved
As mine own father was, art thou by me;
And this impression in my soul abides.
Let but the least among thy people bring
Back to mine ear the tones I heard from thee,
Or should I on the humblest see thy garb,
I will with joy receive him as a god,
Prepare his couch myself, beside our hearth
Invite him to a seat, and only ask
Touching thy fate and thee. Oh, may the gods
To thee the merited reward impart
Of all thy kindness and benignity!
Farewell! Oh, turn thou not away, but give
One kindly word of parting in return!
So shall the wind more gently swell our sails,
And from our eyes with softened anguish flow
The tears of separation. Fare thee well!
And graciously extend to me thy hand,
In pledge of ancient friendship.

How does Thoas respond to this request?
We wait anxiously, together with Iphigenia.
Thoas answers with exactly three words, to wit:

Fare thee well!★

★ Johann Wolfgang von Goethe, "Iphigenia in Tauris," in *The Dramatic Works of Goethe: Including Iphigenia in Tauris, Torquato Tasso, Goetz von Berlichingen, and the Fellow-Culprits*, trans. Anna Swanwick (Boston: S. E. Cassino, 1884), 79–80.

With that, the play is over, and we are alone with the silence that it leaves behind.

The listener experiences something similar when hearing Robert Schumann's song "'Twas in the magic month of May," a *lied* that likewise ends without ending. It's a very short song, based on a text by Heinrich Heine, but the eternal question that it leaves with us has endured from the moment it was composed until today:

> *'Twas in the magic month of May*
> *   When all the buds were springing,*
> *My heart was filled with fervors,*
> *   With dreams, and young Love clinging . . .*

> *'Twas in the magic month of May*
> *   When every bird was singing;*
> *I poured out all the raptures*
> *   With which my heart was ringing.*

Longing knows no limits, and we can hear that in Schumann's song. At the end of the two short verses, the melody isn't resolved by a return to the tonic, instead it ends on the subdominant, an unresolved ending—which is answered in the next song of the cycle, beginning with the line: *Out of my tears and sorrows / The blossoming flowers arise.*[*]

So, without saying a word about the relationship between these short pieces of music, Schumann tells a story, through the music and with the music. In fact, there is a caesura between one piece and the next, but it can only be recognized, or heard, by those who know to listen for it.

---

[*] Heinrich Heine, *Poems of Heinrich Heine*, trans. Louis Untermeyer (New York: Harcourt, Brace, 1916), 45.

And so in silence, in every silence that is not dead and empty, but rather filled to the brim with what is truly essential, literature and music meet. Both literature and music are closely connected to this silence, in their essence they are nothing but interpretations of this silence, at least insofar as they aim to arrive at something like truth. And both music and literature—which creates sounds in our minds, even when we are reading silently—have the privilege that they can take those things that cannot or will not be spoken of directly, and make them audible in other ways.

There was a time in my life, too, when I wanted to study voice alongside my actual area of study, opera directing, because there is really nothing better than being in the *middle* of the music. However, the repertoire I would have been suited for—if I had ever managed to become a soloist at all—was the soubrette, the light, bright soprano, Marzelline in *Fidelio*, Despina in *Così fan tutte*, Ännchen in *Freischütz*, in other words, the handmaids, the so-called "light" repertory. But of course I would have preferred to sing Isolde, so I quickly dropped that plan.

After that, I was actually very happy with my choice of opera directing, and I still am today, since in fact that course of study, as arcane as it may seem, offers a valuable starting point for writing novels and plays. After all, the head that I use to think when I'm writing today is still the same head that I used years ago, as a director, to think about what's *actually* being said when a romantic song is in 4/4 time like a march, or what kind of world it is where Mozart manages to make Pamina and Papageno's pursuers dance and laugh with the help of magic bells. Why is the third with which Wagner accompanies all the characters who make *themselves* invisible with the Tarnhelm unambiguously related to the other third that occurs when Siegfried is slipped a magic potion, causing his *memory* of his wife Brünnhilde to disappear? Or what is Monteverdi telling us—in an opera dedicated to Orpheus, the most famous singer of antiquity, an opera filled with extraordinarily beautiful and complex music—when at the end of that opera the music turns remarkably tedious as Orpheus is being led by his father Apollo—who still views him as a failure—back to his home in the heavens, as if to a prison of bread and water?

And even if I haven't taken the connection between literature and music quite as far as the Austrian author Heimito von Doderer, who titled a cycle of short stories *Divertimenti and Variations*, and another of his short texts *Sonatina* (in which he tells three separate stories that aren't held together at all by their plots, but solely by their rich, nearly musical variations of tempo and character traits), still my work with opera strongly encouraged me to allow myself more freedom in formal terms as well: freedom from the compulsion of realism, freedom to posit a different reality, an affirmation of a sort of artificiality, which—if it is radical enough—can come much closer to life than any "lifelike" depiction or retelling.

After all, what could offer a better education in the principle of collage than the finale of the first act of Mozart's *Don Giovanni*, in which three different pieces of music, played by two small ensembles on stage and by the orchestra in the pit, begin to tumble into each other, at first unnoticeably, then more and more frenetically, until the entire order is brought to collapse—but all of this, of course, in accordance with the rules of art. What capriciousness, but also what a deep truth is to be found in the alternation between the inner sense of time stretching out and the outer reality of time rushing madly onward, the alternation between the pause of an aria, in which thoughts and feelings proliferate, and the rapid advancement of plot in a recitative. And what a gift are sextets, for instance, in which each of the six voices sings in its own way, but still harmonizes with the others.

In an ideal case, my listening allows me, in a flash, to understand an entire world that can stand behind a single sound—though this understanding is by no means necessarily rational.

And in such moments of understanding, it seems to me, music reveals its close kinship with literature—for as a reader, too, I try to trace the many and various interrelations that I encounter in a book.

In my play *Cats Have Nine Lives*, for instance, there are these twelve scenes in which the women are "unleashed" like the beasts in a Roman arena, but between these twelve scenes there is always a brief interlude in which we hear these same women very differently, as the two sides of a single being that has not yet split into two—as we learn in the prologue—struggling with each other.

Those are two entirely different worlds: on the one hand, the dark heavens—in which this being splits into two, out of which this being falls to earth at the beginning of the play, embodied in the two women, and in which each of the interludes takes place—and on the other hand the barren earth, where these two women have to live as humans until they manage to overcome the egoism that has separated them from themselves and cast them down to earth.

So these are the two planes, initially, that stand in conflict with one another and comment on each other. The events that unfold on earth are locked inside a sort of rigid crystalline structure by the interludes that take place in that heavenly no-man's-land, and only at the very end of the play do the women manage to break out of this structure.

But even on the plane of human existence—that is, on earth—the two women meander through various voices, over the course of the twelve scenes they take on twelve very different roles, and each role has its own tone, a young woman speaks differently than a teacher, a lover differently than an old woman. However, the two actresses hold all of these sounds together through their physical presence, their bodies, so that despite all of their differences, the roles remain related to one another.

The third plane is the transformation that takes place within one and the same character, within a single scene. The daughter at the beginning of the scene that I cited above is very clearly a different person than the same daughter at the end, when the mother dies.

And so forth.

So, as you see, we have very different kinds of language here, very different tones, very different voices, that hopefully succeed on various planes at drawing our thoughts along with them, making those thoughts possible.

My starting point for these reflections was an experience that is surely not unique to me, one that will be familiar to you, too: namely, the fact that we ourselves speak in different voices, on different planes, over the course of our lives, often even over the course of a single day, although we continue to think of ourselves as *one* person that entire time; the fact that other "worlds" are continually crossing our paths, spurring us on, disturbing us, maybe rendering us powerless, or at least forcing us in a different direction than we had expected; the experience that we sometimes find ourselves on one side of a given debate at one point in life, and then on the opposite side at another point, often to our own surprise. (And with great conviction both times ...)

So I had plenty of inspiration and material for my *Cats* play, but the fact that I wrote it in this particular way—and the fact that my books *Visitation* and *The End of Days* have a similar structure, in which each individual chapter unfolds more or less chronologically, but the work as a whole consists of multiple planes nested within one another across the chronological divides, and yet all encompassed within a *single* arc—all of that surely has its roots in my engagement with music, which gave me a different view of how things can be placed in relation to one another. After all, music is fundamentally made of two things: air—and time. Music cannot exist except in the division of time and in its audible passing—this thing that we call time, though we know that in its nature it is never anything but a small piece of eternity. This thing that we call time, although by now we have at least some sense that it doesn't really run chronologically, let alone toward a goal.

So a piece of music that we listen to, like a text, can never be more than an intersection, the point at which those things that transcend our horizons intersect with what can be grasped by our own perceptions.

Where does all the time go, asks the Jewish girl in *Visitation*. And in the book *The End of Days*, we read:

But time has blurred all those things that happened for the last time without it being called the last time. At some point her mother had pinned up her hair for her for the last time. At some point she herself had washed the dishes for the last time while her sister sat at the kitchen table doing her homework. At some point she sat in Krasni Mak for the last time. At many points during her life she had done something for the last time without knowing it.[*]

We can't know everything that happens. And we can't capture everything we know in words. As a last musical example of this other world, this world beyond words that music can reveal, here is one of my favorite passages from Wagner's *Lohengrin*, Act I, Scene 2, in which Elsa von Brabant is accused of murdering her little brother, who has suddenly disappeared. She is subjected to an excruciating interrogation, but at first she remains silent, and this silence is the basis for a work that lasts an entire evening.

Elsa enters in a very simple white robe; she remains some time at the back of the stage; then she slowly and very timidly comes forward to the front (center). Women, dressed very simply in white, follow her, but remain

[*] Jenny Erpenbeck, *The End of Days*, trans. Susan Bernofsky (New York: New Directions, 2016), 190.

in the extreme background during the first part of the scene, outside the circle where justice is given.

ALL THE MEN.
Behold! she comes, how grief o'er clouds her!
How like an angel of light her hue!
He who with base suspicion loads her
Must prove his dark surmise is true.

KING.
Art thou she, Elsa of Brabant?
Elsa inclines her head in affirmation.
Wilt thou be judged by me, thy sov'reign Lord?
Elsa turns her head toward the King, looks into his eyes, and then assents with a trusting gesture.
Then further I ask thee:
If the charge to thee is known,
That darkly is alleged against thee?
Elsa looks at Frederick and Ortrud, shudders, inclines her head sadly and assents.
What is your response to the accusation?
Elsa makes a gesture indicating: "Nothing!"
Then thy guilt thou dost confess?

ELSA.
Looks forward sadly for a while.
Oh, my poor brother!

ALL THE MEN.
'Tis wondrous strange—
Her words I cannot fathom.*

---

* Translation adapted from *Wagner's Opera Lohengrin, Containing the German Text, with an English Translation and the Music of All the Principal Airs* (Boston: Oliver Ditson Co., 1890).

Listen to this scene sometime when you have the chance—my favorite recording is the one with Elisabeth Grümmer as Elsa von Brabant, conducted by Rudolf Kempe—and you will understand what opportunities there are in music to make a person's disposition and inner feelings perceptible without the use of words. The alternation between something that is audible, something that is *there*, and something that is silent, is at the core of what we call music. It is what we know from the outset—long before we learn to understand (or misunderstand) each other through the use of words. And even beneath the level of speech, it is always there.

The first rhythm that we can call our own is the heartbeat, it makes our blood flow, makes our veins pulse, then comes birth, and with it, screaming, breathing, blinking, then steps, falling down, getting up again, then crying, then the sounds of pain and happiness course through us, food moves through us, we open ourselves up, as in love, or we close ourselves off, as in hate, we hammer and hit and tear and batter and nod and grab and give and throw and pull and push and roll and jump, and then come curiosity, monotony, and variation, we plant, harvest, sing, or march, there are fights and desires, separations and unions, farewells, secrets, and confessions, we open ourselves up or close ourselves off, and then come children, then come friends, groups of friends, groups of enemies, or no one, then come the complaints, we're too hot or too cold, we're wide awake or dead tired, it's loud all around us, or quiet, we collect, forget, repress, lose, find again, search, get rich, go broke, save, or waste, we go, turn around, run, sink, climb up, get lost, stand still, go astray, we believe in higher powers, we disdain, withdraw, we are free or dependent, implacable, susceptible, or stubborn, we laugh, give up, doubt, we have aims or we're aimless, things work out for us or they go wrong: All of that *is* music, we can easily read it and understand it as music.

And we know that beneath everything that I have just recited, like a counterpoint, is the greatest, lifelong, gradual movement that pervades all of that, our own waxing and waning.

From the moment we come into the world, throughout every single day of our lives, even during the past hour of this lecture, and during the last minute and a half that it has taken me to read this final section, my "aria," that sound is there, that sound that rings out only once in a given lifetime, and it forms the deepest contrasting voice, the voice that underlies everything else that makes up our lives, at every moment, the voice that everything else that we do must be measured against, measures itself against, whether we like it or not, for all time.

EARLY JUNE 2013

Becoming Myself

Ladies and Gentlemen,
Dear Colleagues and Dear Friends,

I was told that in order to introduce myself, I should briefly tell you how I became the person I am, and why I write, in roughly five minutes.

And so I thought about what ought to be included in this speech.

Should I say, must I say, that the tenement building where my grandmother lived, together with my great-grandmother, in an apartment off of the third courtyard back from the street, always smelled like cold ashes from the heating stoves?

Or that my mother once let me skip school to go ice skating on the Liepnitzsee when it was frozen over?

Should I say that my grandmother always gave my mother, and later my mother always gave me, a pot full of food to take home after every visit, with a rubber band stretched from one handle to the other in an X, and the X crossed right at the handle, in the middle of the lid?

Should I say that my white tights always itched when my father's parents took me with them to the theater? That I climbed a birch tree in the ruins of the New Museum to get up to the second floor? That it was only much later, when I was already grown, that I learned that the magnificent red marble in the Mohren Strasse subway station, which was called Otto-Grotewohl-Strasse in East German days, came from the ruins of the Reich Chancellery? Or that the dead end of Leipziger Strasse was always a good place to go roller skating, so close to the wall?

Should I say that my father, sitting at red lights in his Trabi, would entertain me by rocking his body back and forth until the whole car was bobbing up and down in the waves of the asphalt? Or that my grandmother and great-grandmother washed their dishes for many years in two bowls set into a frame that could be pulled out from the kitchen table? That I learned to fish from my grandfather, and could even tear earthworms in half down the middle without batting an eye? Or must I say, should I say instead—truthfully—that there's nothing I like better than reading? That there's nothing I like better than swimming on my back in a lake? That I'm happiest when I'm wandering through the brush with bare legs? That there's nothing more beautiful to me than listening to music? Or that I was shy as a young girl, so shy that I ruined my first date because I couldn't speak? That I would never have wanted to see anyone again if he had read my diary? I might just as well have shown him my kidneys, or my kneecaps underneath the skin, or held a flashlight in my mouth while I kissed him. Did I already mention that my relatives gave me permission to flop down on the rug and suddenly fall asleep during our East–West reunions? That my aunt from the West laughed when she shook out a rag on my grandmother's balcony in the East and the crumbs flew around the nose of the soldier on border patrol down below? That for a long time I thought that my dark blue, pleated Pioneer skirt was my nicest skirt? That I was eleven years old when my great-grandmother was buried. And sixteen when a friend of mine died. That the publisher of my grandmother's books went bankrupt after the fall of the wall. That certain words, like "shopping hall," fell out of use then, too. That the first place I went after that was Vienna, and then Italy, but not Stuttgart, Frankfurt am Main, or Cologne. That things were very hard for my grandmother near the end. That the gray facades, the gaps left by the bombs, the dead ends along the dividing line gradually disappeared, and I could hardly find my way around my own city. That if I had to choose just *one* book to take with me on the run from the apocalypse, it would be Ovid's *Metamorphoses*, and yet I've never even read the entire book from start to finish. What else I might choose to pack is another question. My grandmother and great-grandmother left behind a small house somewhere in what is now Poland, but they saved themselves and a few photos. My grandparents on my father's side left behind a drawing by Käthe Kollwitz and some pieces of Bauhaus furniture when they emigrated to the Soviet Union, but they saved themselves, a tin can of olive oil, and a cigarette-rolling machine. And a child, too, my father. Save the living things and at least write down the rest, if it's too bulky or too heavy to take along, if it doesn't fit in the suitcase, or if it's already gone, lost, forbidden, confiscated, indecent, outdated, stolen, burned, or returned. Maybe you could say it like that. You could also say that times change, and sometimes it's nice to watch it happen, but sometimes it's not so nice. But that's the way it is, and so it makes sense to brace yourself for whatever may come. To look ahead and behind, and up and down, until even in the thick of battle you can take the time to slowly watch everything, even in the thick of it you can withdraw until you're far enough away that you won't lose your center.

I'm very happy to have been elected to this academy, because I hope that I will be able to speak with you about all these things of which language is only the outermost shell.

Thank you very much.

OCTOBER 2014

Hans Fallada

Ladies and Gentlemen, esteemed jury, dear Wend Kässens! In the beginning, Hans Fallada would have liked to be someone other than he really was. "My whole life would have gone differently if I had been able to dance," he once wrote.

Herta Müller once said in a conversation about her youth that she had nearly become a tailor. And she really wouldn't have minded it, either. If she hadn't gone to high school and left her village, there would be a tailor named Herta Müller in Romania today.

So what is the essential thing, then? The thing that gives people the form in which they are most truly themselves?

Fallada began his adult life as the manager of a farm—and not a bad one, either—and he traded in potatoes.

But that wasn't the essential thing.

Why does a person want to write?

I think we want to write because we find it hard to make ourselves understood.

Because we find that things fall by the wayside when we speak.

In fact, as strange as it sounds, the most important reason for writing is probably that we are at a loss for words.

Fallada was addicted to morphine.

Fallada spent time in prison—here in Neumünster, among other places.

He was also one of those men who ran up and down the stairs selling advertisements for a newspaper that didn't share his political views at all—here in Neumünster.

For a long time, Fallada was very poor.

How does the world look when it is seen through the window of a withdrawal clinic, or through the bars of a prison, or from the shores of poverty? Or again: How do you look, in all the various lives contained within your one life? You will never lose that sense of distance, of *indescribable* distance, but still, you can try to describe that shore, the cliffs, everything on the margins of that distance. And then?

Fallada did not offer any bridges in his books.

In the novel *Every Man Dies Alone*, a worker distributes antifascist postcards at great risk to his own life until he is finally caught. He learns as he awaits his sentencing that almost all of these postcards inspired nothing but fear in the people who found them, and were turned in to the authorities immediately. The only person who has been moved to reflection by the worker's stubborn tenacity is the man tasked with pursuing him, the Gestapo commissioner, who ultimately takes his own life. So this book tells of a deed—or better, a doing—and this doing is undone at the end of the book.

So what is this book for?

Words have an astounding ability to transform the air, and just by showing us reality from another perspective, they can transform one reality into another.

Every man dies alone.

But writing conceals within itself a reserve of time.

And a reserve of possibilities.

Fallada is not only the man who writes the forbidden postcards, he is also each person who finds them, who is too afraid to pass them on. He is not only the man who risks his life, but also the man who fails. Fallada clearly knows his way around the dreary apartments of the alcoholics he describes, and it is his own fear that expresses itself in his characters' fears of denunciation and torture.

He never lacked the courage to reveal what he knew, even at his own expense.

But as for what lies in the abyss, he offers only his silence:

Every Man Dies Alone contains not one description of a typical Hitler devotee who remains enthusiastic to the end—someone with an inborn inclination not to evil, but to thoughtlessness, a thoughtlessness that brings with it the capacity for coldness.

But we know: Unfortunately there were many typical Hitler devotees who remained enthusiastic to the end—people with an inborn inclination not to evil, but to thoughtlessness, a thoughtlessness that brought with it the capacity for coldness.

Recently, the principal of a school in Bavaria accidentally cheered on her students in a mousetrap car race by yelling "Sieg Heil!"

Fallada doesn't *want* to believe this.

The abyss confronts him, rendering him mute.

And perhaps it is this muteness, this silence, in which we most clearly see who Fallada is.

The first book of Fallada's that I read, when I was still a child, was his wonderful collection *Stories from Miniland*. In one of those stories, a horse lies buried in ice throughout the entire winter, frozen alive, in suspended animation, so to speak.

Everyday fascism was a thick layer of ice.

Fallada is actually the name of a horse; the author's pen name was borrowed from an animal in one of the Grimms' fairy tales.

And then along came Johannes R. Becher, who wanted to *thaw him out*—for a new era that was supposed to be different.

But the new era didn't last very long for the man named Fallada. Just two years.

Lying under the ice that long had taken a lot of strength.

Sometimes it is too late for certain lives.

There is nothing worse, it seems to me, than when it is too late for something that we wish for so strongly.

That, fundamentally, is why I wrote the book for which I was invited here today.

If I had one wish—it would be to believe in the many possibilities of surviving death.

I thank you for strengthening me in my wishes with this very lovely prize.

MARCH 2014

"Will I Come to a Miserable End?"
On Thomas Mann

ACCEPTANCE SPEECH FOR THE THOMAS MANN PRIZE
OF THE HANSEATIC CITY OF LÜBECK AND THE
BAVARIAN ACADEMY OF FINE ARTS

Ladies and Gentlemen, esteemed jury, honorable mayor, dear Michael Krüger, dear Knut Elstermann—and dear family!

It means a great deal to me to receive this prize that is named for Thomas Mann, an author I love and greatly admire.

I have received congratulations from all sides, I am thrilled to see my name linked in this way to the name of this great writer, and of course I am also happy about the prize money, which is nothing to scoff at.

And even though my affinity for Thomas Mann's work is hardly enough in itself to justify this honor, I would like to make an attempt here to describe this affinity, and to address some points that connect me to Thomas Mann's work.

When I was a teenager, I would ask my father year after year if I could finally read *The Magic Mountain*, but year after year my father would give me something else to read instead, something by Adalbert Stifter or Laurence Sterne, because he thought *The Magic Mountain* might still be "too difficult." Eventually I got the impression that it must be a real magic mountain of some kind, too strenuous for a mere teenager to climb, or perhaps some sort of "open sesame" that would reveal its secrets only to a grown woman. So when I finally did open the book, setting foot for the first time in the world of that reputedly serious, difficult magic mountain, I was initially taken aback. The enchanting Madame Chauchat slammed the door with a crash, and I found myself captivated by her—and laughing as I read. Next I turned to Mann's stories, discussing them passionately with my best friend at the time, considering all sorts of questions: Did my naturally blonde hair and healthy constitution make me better suited to the vulgar daytime world than to the wonderful nighttime world of a Gabriele Eckhof? To what extent did one need a character defined by suffering and melancholy—ideally recognizable even from afar—if one hoped to create *good and true* art? But while these considerations troubled me, my worries were assuaged on every page, as Thomas Mann gazed from a judicious distance upon all the techniques that people use to regulate their interactions with others, training his great wisdom upon everything that takes place beneath those superficial vanities.

I made these first forays into Thomas Mann's works before I began studying to be an opera director; in other words, before I discovered how Wagner's universe is fragmented into a daytime and a nighttime world, before I anachronistically recognized Thomas Mann's leitmotif technique in Wagner's, before I yielded to the intoxications of *Parsifal* and *Tristan* myself—retroactively, as it were. Thomas Mann's concern with the temporal structure of music continues to inform my thoughts—and my writing!—to this day; for instance, the question of the complex relationship between movement and stasis that "occupied" Adrian Leverkühn "more than anything else": the "transformation of the intervals into a chord . . . , of the horizontal, that is, into the vertical, of the sequential into the simultaneous."*

The inevitable question of literary role models is a tedious one that ultimately misses the mark, but of course we do recognize ourselves at times in the language and thoughts of others, and in happy moments of reading we become aware of something that cor*responds* to us. And even if we forget certain details over the

* Thomas Mann, *Doctor Faustus*, trans. John E. Woods (New York: Knopf, 1997), 244.

years—a given story line or character—and even if we remember certain others; the most important things sink in deeper than our memories, we internalize them, take them into our bodies, and they stay there, blind and mute, like our hearts, our kidneys, our bones, keeping us alive.

Between finishing Mann's *Magic Mountain* and starting to read his *Doctor Faustus*, I lost the country I came from—the GDR. In the course of that time, I internalized Mann's reflections on all that is doomed to decline, his uncompromisingly accurate representations of illness and in-between states and all the things that occupy us when we are in those states. Hans Castorp lies on the chaise longue, professionally swaddled in blankets, increasingly resigned to his illness, while already his time is trickling away (but only we readers know that), running toward the First World War as if in a countdown, faster and faster. The slower life seems to become, the more quickly the moment approaches in which everything that had existed up to that point will be irreversibly lost on the battlefields. Thomas Mann succeeds in inverting the order of farce and tragedy. One moment we're enjoying a civilized lunch, then comes the mustard gas. And after the First World War comes the Treaty of Versailles, followed in short order by the food shortages in Europe, the inflation, the age of dictatorships: in Italy, in Yugoslavia, in Poland, in the Soviet Union, in Spain, and finally in Germany. Hitler is essentially a belated response to Versailles. After a few years of in-between time, Hitler answered one war with another, far surpassing the first by systematically murdering a portion of Germany's own civilian population along with millions of people in other countries, even those who lived far from the front.

Anyone who could understand how an end becomes a beginning, how a beginning in turn becomes an end again, would surely also understand that fundamental thing, the principle of transformation: how something unknown can emerge from what we thought we knew; how one thing can be swallowed up by another, very different thing—how it can be inverted, transformed into something monstrous, no longer controllable—or sometimes (just as surprising, though significantly more pleasant), into beauty, new life, new form. Anyone who understood that in all its depth could more easily cope with hopes that come to nothing; or with the loss of one's own power, whether through political caprice, the actions of rivals, sickness, or the rise of the next generation; could more easily accept what is so difficult to accept: the deaths of those close to us—and our own deaths, which put an end to the thought process by which we seek to comprehend death until the moment when it finally catches up to us.

Even now we find ourselves in one of those in-between states. We know that the causes of the wars and crises in the Arab world, in Afghanistan, or in the Ukraine, can ultimately be traced back to the collapse of the Eastern Bloc, which occurred a full 25 years ago. In many places—both within Europe and on its periphery—these developments are currently contributing to a radicalization that might remind us in some respects of the radicalization of the 1920s. Orbán is building fences, severing his connections to European politics, and impatience is also growing in other countries, not least in our own. A dictatorship has already been established in Turkey. Erdoğan's approach is so similar to Hitler's in 1933—which we can trace day by day in Thomas Mann's diary—that the parallels are almost uncanny. In February 1933, Thomas Mann's friends advised him not to return to Munich from Switzerland, where he was enjoying a winter vacation after a reading tour. After that, one thing led to another. When his passport expired in April, the German authorities declined to renew it; his German bank accounts, his house in Munich, and his cars were confiscated, and with them half of his Nobel Prize was out the window; so in just a few weeks the most honorable Thomas Mann, practically a pillar of the state, was transformed into a refugee who did not know where to go. He wrote: "It is hard for me to bear the uncertainty of the future, this improvised life, the absence of any firm foundations that would, at least subjectively, remain valid forever, unto death. That is exactly what I have lost, and it is surely no surprise that a replacement cannot be found in the blink of an eye.... Will I come to a miserable end?" He also wrote: "Very anxious, depressed, dreary mood. Must acknowledge that fundamentally there is no getting used to the loss of one's home and of a stable livelihood." As he would later learn, records had been kept of his public statements since 1925. In that in-between period, in the shadows, as it were, something was growing that would suddenly emerge and would thoroughly, permanently throw his life off course overnight.

A sentence from *Mario and the Magician*, which I read as a young girl, has stayed in my memory all these years. It goes:

"It is likely that not willing is not a practicable state of mind; *not* to want to do something may be in the long run a mental content impossible to subsist on. Between not willing a certain thing and not willing at all—in other words, yielding to another person's will—there may lie too small a space for the idea of freedom to squeeze into."*

When it comes to willing—or the formulation of a wish *to will*—dictators have an advantage over democratic countries. In Europe, we can agree on what we *don't* want, at least not here in our own countries: war, poverty, torture. But what we *do* want is a question that requires more consideration. The very big,

* Thomas Mann, "Mario and the Magician," in *Death in Venice, Tonio Kröger, and Other Writings*, ed. Frederick Alfred Lubich, trans. H. T. Lowe-Porter (New York: Continuum, 1999), 82.

but also very capacious, word "freedom" is not enough. First of all, because we have to ask: Whose freedom? And at whose expense? Second of all, because it requires us to take a step back from *willing as such*, to take back our own wishes, when in doubt, in the interest of equality. At this point, the freedom to which we so often appeal contains within itself the seeds of its own destruction. "Freedom is always the freedom of those who think differently," the brilliant Rosa Luxemburg said, and there's the rub, if we're honest. Consumption is a constant process that offers the soul no satisfaction in the long run. Consumption is also a predatory process, a matter of life and death for people elsewhere. Taken together, these two facts mean that things can't stay as they are. We are in an in-between state, and it will be important to understand what is growing there and where we are heading, where it is our *will* to go, before we are robbed of the ability to will anything at all.

All of these considerations confront us with the very central question of borders. Not only the borders between one country and another, or between one continent and another, but above all the borders within ourselves. Between ourselves as egoistic individuals and ourselves as members of a community in which we depend on one another, a community which, in light of the economic and ecological interdependence of all continents in our present era, can only reasonably be considered as a global community. Our *own* desires, too, sometimes transgress against the agreed-upon order or the law, posing the question: Are we criminals? Or do we have to insist on these desires, in the interest of further progress? Such a law may ultimately prove inappropriate, it may have already *become* inappropriate, or it may rest on a misunderstanding, like the marriage between Isolde and Marke. Often enough, laws are purely arbitrary, the laws themselves are criminal. Do we lose ourselves, or do we save ourselves precisely by respecting borders, by insisting on them?

So: Is a border a constraint or a support? Of course it is always both, to a certain extent.... But there is no law to relieve us of the duty to judge for ourselves. At that point, we are always on our own again.

Thomas Mann's humor and his uncompromising portraits would have been unthinkable if he had not already looked upon his own society from a tremendous distance, even long before he was expelled from it in 1933. It was his job, so to speak, to know what it means to be "outside." That is at the root of Adrian Leverkühn's entire bargain: The price that he pays for his art is that even in moments of happiness, reflection makes him a stranger. On the other hand, there is the power of feeling, the uncompromising will, the ruthlessness that he shows toward both himself and others. To be a drifter, an outcast, an untouchable in a no-man's-land, in an inhospitable territory, always engaged in an intimate dialogue with borders. What courage it took to have Aschenbach whisper his profession of love for the young boy shortly before his death in Venice, to have him confess the feeling that should not have been there, but was there nonetheless. Aschenbach is alone in his room when he makes this confession, but Thomas Mann was revealing himself to the thousands of readers he already had at the time, not least of all to his wife Katia. Isolde commits adultery. Aschenbach's pederastic desire remains unrealized. But feeling and desire lead both characters to cross a border. And feeling and desire are, after all, the signs that someone is alive. Never more alive than in the face of death.

SEPTEMBER 2016

Ovid's "Metamorphoses"

SPEECH FOR THE PREMIO STREGA EUROPEO

Still, love clings to the spurned girl and grows on grief. / Sleepless and anxious, she begins to waste away; / Her skin shrivels and her body dries up, until / Only her voice and bones are left, and then / Only her voice. They say her bones turned into stone. / She hides in the woods, and is seen no more in the hills / But can be heard by all, and lives on as sound. [*]

In his *Metamorphoses*, Ovid tells the story of how the nymph Echo is transformed into something immaterial, how her body, unloved by Narcissus, falls away, in exchange for an eternity as sound.

I first encountered this book in school. Like generations of students before me, I attempted to translate the beginning of the book, the chapter about the four ages. But I didn't really read it until much later, and ever since then, I've *read around* in it again and again, to put it more accurately, since it isn't the kind of book you read from front to back at a single go. The book itself seems to be in motion, it's convoluted, and since I'm cursed with a poor memory, I always have to begin by reorienting myself to the tangle of the gods' names, I have to remind myself of the relationships and connections between the chapters. And I'm always finding things in the book that I wasn't even looking for, I run aground here and there, discover this or that new territory. And so this book itself almost seems to me like a living thing, something that leads me, responds to me, asks me questions, meets me again and again over the course of my own metamorphoses, in the various ages of life.

---

[*] Ovid, *Metamorphoses*, trans. Stanley Lombardo (Indianapolis: Hackett, 2010), 77.

A metamorphosis can come at the end of a painful journey, like the metamorphosis of the nymph Echo, unhappy in love: Her disappearance is her own doing. Marsyas, who takes on Apollo with his flute in a musical competition and loses, wails as his skin is stripped away as punishment for his hubris: "Why are you tearing me / Out of myself?"* His blood becomes the river Marsyas. But transformation can also take the form of flight and rescue, as is the case with Philomela and her sister, who are caught up in a horrible tale of abuse and revenge until finally, transformed into birds, they escape. Transformation can occur out of love, as in the case of the two ancient lovers Philemon and Baucis, or out of grief, in the case of Niobe, who turns to stone after the gods murder all of her children to punish her for her pride. Metamorphosis can conceal and protect—or punish. It takes away the life someone has known, and, at least in Ovid's telling, it offers eternity in return, omnipresence in another form—a human being becomes sound, becomes stone, water, or tree, becomes animal. And becomes an example to us, the readers, through this metamorphosis, in this newly attained immortality.

But Ovid is not just concerned with human, or human-like, protagonists. For in telling their stories, he also tells the origins of the animals, stones, plants, rivers, air, sound—as if telling a creation story in reverse. He shows us how all things, all substances, all creatures, are intertwined with one another. In the very moment when we lose ourselves as human beings, he sees us as the beginning of something else that lies outside of us and yet contains us. You could also say: In the moment when a river gushes forth, when this or that bird takes flight, when a tree begins to stretch out its branches, in that moment the essential thing begins.

* Ovid, 160.

But whether you look at things from one side or the other, Ovid knows that every static state preserves within itself the process of its own becoming, that movement is contained within the things themselves, in the form of waiting. In his stories, possibility and memory find a refuge alongside each other and with each other. And he knows: Only when we speak of metamorphoses does that which is lost retain its identity.

Ovid himself lived, read, and wrote in a time of transition. In retrospect, we can read his *Metamorphoses*, which he wrote shortly after the birth of Christ, and before he himself was exiled to what is now Romania, as a compendium of everything that had been recorded up to that time in the realm of classical literature and philosophy. We must imagine Ovid in the first place as a reader himself: reading the texts of the ancient Greeks, most notably Homer, who lived 800 years earlier, or Hesiod, 700 years back. Then Pythagoras, Plato, Herodotus—all of whom had been dead for close to 500 years by Ovid's time. The development of writing gives the reader centuries and millennia to reflect. New interpretations can be understood and compared to the original, since they are also transformations of that same material.

Ovid incorporated the stories of all of those "ancients" into his own book, along with some stories of his contemporaries. Greek gods, Roman gods, farmers, warriors, nymphs, demigods, sirens, even Caesar and Augustus—the last of whom would soon banish Ovid from Rome—all of these figures inhabit his *Metamorphoses*. And in his eyes all of these figures become related to one another, for they are all shown in moments of transition. That is a spectacular farewell to half a millennium of democracy, immediately before Augustus installed a monarchy and society was transformed.

Two thousand years later, when we seem to be living in another time of transition, we can delve into Ovid's experiences as we read, we can ask ourselves what is coming.

Growth, as we read in Ovid, is a transformation, but not a forward movement.

We ourselves are the other.

We ask ourselves, with Ovid: What is the essential thing that survives all of these transformations? Who were we, and who will we be? How long will this transition take, how long will we have to wait? Will we lose something if we turn back to the past—as Orpheus loses his Eurydice? Is forgetting our only salvation? Or are our stories the only baggage that no one can take away from us? *Are* we our stories? Just some letters on paper that become flesh anew for each reader. A universe that finds a new home again and again in the mind of everyone who reads it.

Page by page, it all takes place in silence.

And when we die?

Nothing keeps its own shape, and Nature renews / By recycling one form into another. Nothing dies, believe me, in the world as a whole / But only changes its looks. What we call birth / Is a new beginning of what was before, / As death is an ending of a former state.*

JUNE 2017

* Ovid, 425.

Walter Kempowski's Novel *"All for Nothing"*

AN INTRODUCTION

January 1945. The Red Army is advancing into East Prussia. In this icy winter, nearly 750,000 people seek to flee from the front and make their way west via two tongues of land on the Baltic coast—the Curonian Spit and the Vistula Spit. 300,000 of them will lose their lives in the attempt. They freeze to death, they starve, their refugee columns are fired on by airplanes, they sink, together with their horses and wagons, through the ice of the frozen lagoon, the ships that they board in search of safety are sunk by Soviet submarines. The story of this flight is one of the most dramatic chapters in the end of the Second World War, as far as German civilians are concerned.

One of the last ships that shuttles between Rostock and the East Prussian coast, rescuing desperate refugees, is the *Friedrich*. The proprietor is Karl Georg Kempowski. His son, Walter Kempowski, is 15 years old when he sees the East Prussian refugees, nearly dead from exhaustion, disembark in Rostock and "shuffle" through the city. A short time later, he will learn that his father, who was drafted into the Wehrmacht as an officer, has been killed in battle on the Vistula Spit in the final days of the war.

Walter Kempowski himself—born in 1929 and raised in the coastal city of Rostock, which was nearly bombed out of existence by the British in 1942—barely manages to escape the final Battle of Berlin, where he is serving as a courier for the Luftwaffe. In 1948, he and his older brother are sentenced by the Soviet occupying forces to twenty-five years in prison for cooperating with American intelligence; he serves eight years. His mother, accused of complicity, serves six years. At the age when other young men are learning a trade, Kempowski has this prison for a school. In prison he learns to listen. When he's released, East Germany is already seven years old. He is immediately deported to the West, where he studies pedagogy and begins to work as a teacher. And to write. With his preternatural ability to see through political manipulation of all stripes, Kempowski will remain a singular figure in the German literary landscape until he writes his final book.

From the very beginning of his literary career, he works with autobiographical material, but he always regards himself as a source for better understanding history. This principle is at the core of his unsentimental, extraordinarily precise style, which allows and enables the reader to evaluate what is read. This principle is also at the origin of Kempowski's burning interest in discovering other sources of the same kind. While publishing one novel after another, he also places ads in major daily newspapers to solicit diary entries, letters, and photographs. In the end, he assembles an archive of over 8,000 documents and 100,000 photographs, to which he dedicates entire rooms of his house.

These eyewitness accounts that he assembles—in all their intensity and abundance—give rise to a major project, *Sonar*. This ten-volume "collective diary" of selected periods in the Second World War is published between 1993 and 2005: a monumental collage of writings by undistinguished private persons as well as famous writers, politicians, and artists. "To annihilate the experiences of entire generations is an act of wastefulness that we cannot afford," he writes in his foreword to the project. Just as sonar is used to sound the depths of the ocean in navigation, Kempowski sounds the depths of history with these various voices. History as the product of countless individual perspectives. A starving, louse-ridden Russian soldier's letter to his fiancée appears there alongside Himmler's instructions for maintaining the medicinal herb garden in the concentration camp at Dachau, the description of a rollicking family party appears alongside an entry about a Jewish woman's suicide, a memo from Hitler's personal doctor about a daily injection appears alongside a reflection by the antifascist Sophie Scholl about God's goodness. "*Sonar*," Kempowski writes, "belongs to those who patiently attend to the voices in the stratosphere. Listening can make it possible for us at last to come to terms with one another. Whoever seeks an explanation for the ebbing course of mankind may drag one from the depths with *Sonar*."

This life's work provides the background against which Kempowski's final novel, *All for Nothing*, can be read.

A manor house in East Prussia, paid for by the military salary of the absent owner, an officer. Inside, a Chekhovian personage—the lady of the manor, a languorous Berlin beauty—along with her twelve-year-old son Peter, his tutor, an elderly aunt who oversees the household, two Ukrainian maidservants, and a Polish groom who tends the horses. A Nazi lives in the new settlement across the way. The first refugees driven westward from the Baltic territories by the advancing front turn in for a few nights at the manor. We watch along with Kempowski as this old world, as if in slow motion, begins to sway. The Baltic refugees are delighted by the bread with sausage that is still served to them here, they mourn for their lost homeland, they move on. The Polish groom is already beginning to prepare the coach, to pack a few suitcases for his master's family. But the lady of the manor gazes out the window, the son looks through his microscope, the tutor speaks of Goethe's concept of "perfection." How long does it take us to notice the end of the world? To notice that the end of the world might mean our own end?

For his novel, Kempowski draws on his rich collection of private diaries and biographical writings from this region, from this time. There are few works that recount the exodus of the East Prussian Germans with such intensity and precision. And yet *All for Nothing* is neither a novel of expulsion drenched in nostalgia for the lost homeland, nor a rendering of its characters' fear of the Russians, much less a battle painting. Kempowski's art lies in his ability to gaze without prejudice on the desperation, the grief, the hopes, and the egoism of each one of his protagonists—and in doing so, he enables us to sense the weight of such end times, beyond all political partisanship.

The book was originally meant to be called *Twins* and to center on a pair of siblings who flee together at the end of the war, but then Kempowski changed his mind. In his writing journal from 2004, he notes of the character Peter: "Now I see him plodding westward alone." In the final draft of the novel, the sister is already dead when the story begins, but her absence sets a dark tone for the entire book. The suppressed grief for the sister and the shadow cast by the girl's uncertain paternity might remind a German reader of the trauma of the bombing war—that experience that was collectively repressed by the whole of German society, whose megalomania had ended in failure.

So Kempowski's choice of the title *All for Nothing* shifted the focus: from the fate of the individual to the fundamental question of why.

Walter Kempowski's readers had already encountered the words "all for nothing" at a prominent point in his novel *Marrow and Bone*, which appeared in the early nineties. In that novel, a young man from Hamburg, on a business trip in present-day Poland, finds the spot where his father was killed in battle. "All for nothing! ALL FOR NOTHING! He didn't mean the death of his mother or of his father ..., but the suffering of all creatures, the flesh lashed to the stake, the calf he had seen bound and gagged, the torture chamber in the Marienburg, the shuffling procession of mankind beneath the condemning sky. It's all for nothing, he thought, again and again. And: Who's to blame?"*

"All for nothing": By choosing these same words as the title of his final book, Kempowski not only takes up once again the motif of *vanitas*, the question of the meaning and possibilities of all human action, he also returns in this narrative to East Prussia, to that landscape burdened with the death of his own father. Does this bring the circle to a close? Or is the author simply setting out once more to make mute fate speak, to make deaf people hear?

"Wherefrom? Whereto?" These questions recur time and again as a leitmotif throughout the book: sometimes posed in the jaunty tone of the wanderer, sometimes in earnest, still other times with a hint of irony—but always asking after what is truly essential. Kempowski, already approaching the age of 80 as he writes this book, sees himself confronted with his own finitude and thus with the question of what part of himself, of his work, of his reflections will be carried on, will occupy the thoughts of others, will remain. When asked about his choice of the title *All for Nothing* in a 2006 interview, he says: "Sometimes I think that it stands as a motto over all the years of my work...." The bitter reckoning of a man whose success with the public earned him the mistrust of German literary critics, a man whose unerring clarity of vision was mistaken for humor even when it was far from light-hearted, and was thus ironed flat.

But his reflections in this book, in their profundity, go far beyond this personal dimension. Here he poses the question, one final time, of the freedom of humans to act, caught as they are

* Walter Kempowski, *Marrow and Bone*, trans. Charlotte Collins (New York: New York Review Books, 2020), 161.

in a stranglehold between contingency and guilt. The essence of the literary work of an entire lifetime is brought to bear here against the traumatic experiences of a childhood and youth lived during the war, when the adolescent had to learn that in the rain of bombs one house is hit, the other is not, that one 15-year-old is left lying on the battlefield, the other survives, that one prisoner knows why he is sitting in prison, while the other's arrest is due entirely to a misunderstanding in the turmoil that follows the war.

Under the title *All for Nothing*, Walter Kempowski asks one last time: Can one individual accomplish anything? Or does humanity fail again and again, generation after generation, succumbing to forgetting and repression, to contingency, to caprice? Are we moving at all—or are we forever frozen in what we call "history," even as it plays out in our cities, in our lives, in our flesh?

Thus, when he turns his attention to the old, ostensibly ideal days of peace, Kempowski searches there for evidence that even in everyday indifference, even in ordinary envy, even in commonplace acts of concealment, something monstrous lies dormant which, when unleashed by the war, will abolish all the familiar rule books, leaving refugees homeless as they search for meaning. Are we at least guilty of what befalls us? This question hangs over the psychological subtleties that Kempowski details: whether it be the peculiar coldness and detachment that precedes their departure, or the decision made by the lady of the manor to offer a Jewish refugee shelter for the night. Whether it be the subtly homoerotic qualities of the tutor's relationship to his pupil, or the family's repression of their daughter's premature death. In a masterfully choreographed circle dance composed of refugees' tales, of unspoken observations that cast light on one another, of clichés and proverbs strewn throughout the text, of songs, verses, and lines of poetry, Kempowski sees down to the root of things, but that root is different for each character—he brings to bear the entire art of storytelling before he exposes these people, in whose souls all of these things have taken place, to the indifference of the final, icy winter of the war.

In this way, he also pushes narrative realism to its limits. He drives his plot into the arms of the war, the great destroyer of stories. Faced with the physical annihilation of human beings, which, after all, is not least the annihilation of memories, of relationships and hopes, he not only asks after the purpose of storytelling, he also asks who will even be left to pass on these episodes as a living legacy, to spin these tales further, through his own life, into the present and the future. Does Kempowski himself only inspect what is being destroyed? Or might he tell these stories in order to feed this destruction? The irony of the writer's craft is that when loss is recounted, what is lost is preserved.

Young Peter, the only character in the novel who is catapulted out of the old world into the new, carries under his arm the microscope that he only recently used to examine the blood that flowed from the body of his deceased aunt. This boy would have encountered us again in a text that Kempowski left as an unpublished fragment with the working title "A Little Love of Trumpets," in which Peter works as a restorer in 2007 Berlin. What does a restorer do? He recreates what once was—and does so with the greatest of care, devoting the very same care to reconstructing both the beauty and the flaws of times gone by. Because understanding is only possible, if at all, when we have a view of the whole.

"Peter is me, of course, a second, a multiple self-portrait. Otherwise I wouldn't have been able to write the book."

Walter Kempowski, whose death in 2007 tore him away from his work, bids farewell to his readers with this novel in which the survival of the young Peter, his *alter ego*, appears not like reality, but like a wish transformed into literature.

"Was everything all right now?" is the final sentence of the book—a sentence, it's said, that Kempowski long hesitated to write.[*]

JULY 2017

---

[*] Walter Kempowski, *All for Nothing*, trans. Anthea Bell (New York: New York Review Books, 2018), 343.

SOCIETY

How Are You? Good?

AN OBITUARY FOR BASHIR ZAKARYAU

In a small apartment in Berlin, a powerful man is lying on the floor. He is covered in bedsheets. Bashir Zakaryau is dead.

He survived the unrest in Nigeria, where his father was burned to death. He survived the war in Libya, where black Africans were hunted openly on the street. When the boat that he was forced onto by Gaddafi's people capsized, his five-year-old daughter and three-year-old son, who were below deck, drowned. Bashir held on to a rope and survived the death of his children.

In this way, he made it to Lampedusa, and then to the Italian mainland. There was no work.

He came to Germany. There, under the Dublin II Regulation, he was not allowed to work.

Bashir, who first had a metalsmith's shop in Nigeria, and then started all over again in Libya, knew what it meant not to be allowed to work.

If you aren't allowed to work, you can never really arrive.

If you aren't allowed to work, you remain trapped in your own memories.

If you aren't allowed to work, your own hopes are your enemy.

When African refugees set up a protest camp in 2012 on Oranienplatz in Berlin to draw attention to the inhumanity of Europe's asylum policies, Bashir started to speak for his people.

No one who heard him speak will ever forget him. He was loud, he was passionate, he understood that great power is required to set things in motion, but also that motion means working with each other, not against each other. He understood that the Dublin regulations had deepened the divides. He was a powerful figure, but he abhorred violence. "I can't see any more blood," he told me in one of the conversations that I had with him for my last book. He wanted parity, equal rights, he wanted to bring visibility to the invisible, to the people who had been suppressed from the public consciousness. There were demonstrations, meetings, interviews. But the Senate didn't want to set a precedent. Bashir, a statesman without a state, was never received by Berlin's state minister of the interior.

Bashir survived for two years in a tent on Oranienplatz. Two summers, two winters. For the young men whose fathers had been murdered, he was a father. For the silent—those who had lost their voices amid the horrors of their flight—he was a voice. And for those who were only concerned with their own welfare, he was the one who taught them to see themselves as members of a community.

When the Senate finally proposed a so-called "agreement" and made vague promises to the men, Bashir signed on all their behalf. It's hard when your own hope is your enemy.

The group was divided among three shelters; suddenly, they were transformed into so many "individual cases" to be examined. "How are you? Good?" Bashir hoped. Bashir laughed. Bashir, the giant, wore a t-shirt with a skeleton printed on it. Never has there been a skeleton with so much flesh. Bashir transformed anyone he hugged into a child. Bashir explained the five pillars of Islam to me, saying: "Anyone who kills is not a Muslim. You may not even kill the smallest animal, because it may be that that animal has children waiting for it at home."

Bashir organized community service, so that the young men who were spending years of their lives waiting would have something to do. They raked leaves. They cleaned preschools. He was the one who took care of all of those people who had been shut out of society, the one who lifted them up, gave them courage, comforted them, consoled them. In the meantime, the information tent on Oranienplatz, the old meeting point, had been set on fire by unknown people for the second time. "Hi, how are you? Good?" Whenever Bashir, the metalsmith, saw a railing, a gate, a grate, he would say: "This was my work. I can make this. This was my work."

Bashir was granted a "temporary stay" on account of his heart disease, and moved into a different home. When his mother called to ask how he was doing, he would say: "Good." Sometimes he didn't answer the telephone anymore. He said: "My mother is very sick. I would like to see her again before she dies." But the doctors told him that he wouldn't survive the flight.

Aside from a few exceptions on account of illness, the "individual cases" were sent back to Italy by the immigration authorities, as required by law. Bashir was not allowed to take in his friends who were now homeless. One friend would call, then another, then another. Bashir said: "It kills me. I'm in the shelter and my brothers are being put out on the street." He got worked up, and had to leave the shelter. His possessions: two suitcases and a few bags of things. A respirator to use at night. A plastic bag of medications. A folder of letters from government offices.

His new accommodations were in the rear house of a rundown Berlin apartment building that was also being operated as a "shelter" for refugees. Bashir—in his early forties, a former entrepreneur, former father, the political leader of the Oranienplatz group—wasn't allowed to have visitors there at night. No friends, whether men or women. There was a curfew from 10 at night until 11 in the morning. One morning, when the landlord checked the rooms at 6, he found one of Bashir's homeless friends hiding in the closet, another under the bed, a third in the bath.

Bashir had to leave that shelter, too. It was getting close to Christmas.

And right then, the offer of another apartment came down

from heaven. One and a half rooms. The first apartment of his own after five years of flight.

In the months that followed, Bashir would take in two brothers—one with a wife and two small children—and a young student. Not one after the other, but all at once. He also helped his friends who had gone to Italy to renew their papers, piling their suitcases in his apartment. The landlords, true angels, knew that he couldn't say no, and they smiled.

A few weeks ago he told me: I would like so much to have children again.

Now he's lying in his apartment, covered in bedsheets.

There's still no solution in sight for his people.

The long battle that he fought for his people is over, but only for him. In the end, survival was more than Bashir Zakaryau could survive. But it wasn't Bashir who gave up, it was only his heart.

OCTOBER 2016

Blind Spots

Dear Ladies and Gentlemen,

I'm very pleased to speak to you today, particularly since so many fundamental questions that have been hibernating in some blind spot of our consciousness for the past two decades have recently taken on an unaccustomed urgency. Many concepts have suddenly become acute, as it were, and it might be worthwhile to consider their meaning once again from a fresh perspective. One of these concepts, of course, is that of the border—along with the concepts of transition and transgression, in the sense of border crossing. Closely related to these is the concept of freedom.

I was in my early twenties when the Berlin Wall fell and the country where I had grown up disappeared in the course of just a few weeks. Every East German could go to the West to receive 100 "Westmarks," known as "welcome money," and six months later the transition to the West German currency marked the official "reunification"—in other words, the end of the German Democratic Republic, nowadays called East Germany, and the expansion of the German Federal Republic. From that moment on, anyone could say whatever he wanted about the former head of state Erich Honecker, or the Stasi head Erich Mielke—or even about the West German chancellor, Helmut Kohl!—and anyone could travel to Paris, Venice, or New York. While people were still celebrating this new "software," as we might call it today, drastic changes were taking place in the "hardware" as well. A public trust sold a number of East German factories for literally one mark to West German companies, which closed them shortly thereafter. Many workers lost their jobs, and university professors, lecturers, and researchers were also laid off in the East and replaced by university professors, lecturers, and researchers from the West. When the common currency was introduced, rents increased by a factor of 10 overnight. West German speculators bought up East German real estate, and state-owned enterprises were privatized. The so-called new federal states were transformed into an enormous market, where all sorts of things could be successfully sold—as we've seen, not just bananas. Suddenly everyone was talking about money. Wait, we could talk about money? Shocking.

Ever since then, there has been a border between the two halves of my life: a border made of time, between the first half of my life, which was transformed into history by the fall of the wall and the collapse of the East German state, and the second half, which began at that same moment. Without this experience of transition, from one world to a very other one, I probably never would have started writing. That much is clear to me today. My writing began with reflections on borders, reflections on how we change over the course of our lives, voluntarily or involuntarily, reflections on what identity is, and how much we can lose without losing ourselves.

I had known this border all my life, but when it disappeared in 1989, it went very quickly. Why did it go so quickly? Because we East and West Germans shared a language? Because we, or some of us at least, had families that spanned the East / West divide? "Blood relatives"? Because the works of Goethe and Schiller were taught in schools on both sides of the wall?

Why did people always pronounce the word "freedom" with such enthusiasm, as they continue to do today, whenever they speak of the collapse of East Germany, whereas when people from other countries strive for freedom—from countries like Mali, Niger, Afghanistan, Pakistan, Mexico, Haiti, and other "shitholes," as Donald Trump recently described them—they're met with contempt and aversion?

Why do we still see pictures on TV every year on the anniversary of the fall of the wall, showing happy East Germans jubilantly sitting astride the wall—whereas pictures of people scaling the twenty-foot barbed-wire fence that separates the Spanish enclave of Melilla from Morocco only inspire tougher security measures from the European Union?

Why do we still hear laments for the Germans who died attempting to flee over the wall but almost none for the countless refugees who have drowned in the Mediterranean in recent years, turning the sea into a giant grave? Why is it that the opening of the border in 1989 was something wonderful, but today voices cry out for new and stronger borders? What is the difference between these two groups of people who aspire to a new life, to this thing we call "freedom"?

The answer is: nothing.

But there is another answer, too: The difference is the history of these groups and the significance attached to these events.

Seen from the West, the collapse of the Eastern Bloc marked the victorious end of the Cold War, and the fall of the Berlin Wall signified the failure of Communist ideals and utopias. The bankruptcy of any economic system that rejected profit motives could be seen in the parade of Trabis, those iconic East German cars that made their way to West Berlin the night that the wall fell. By contrast, the images of the Spanish enclave of Melilla, the televised images of overcrowded refugee boats, and the designs for the Mexican border wall tell very different stories: stories of postcolonial exodus and of the one-way street of globalization, a system in which European and North American countries, and more recently China, move money around the world, forming alliances with the corrupt elites of other nations to exploit their raw materials, often with the aid of war and violence, while refusing to accept the people who flee from these exploited nations, viewing them as a sort of waste product unwelcome "on our shores."

True, the Geneva Convention defines the term "refugee," and the countries that signed this convention agreed to guarantee the right of asylum to political refugees, for example. It's a good thing, a very good thing, that Germany fixed this right in its constitution. Nevertheless, the relevant paragraph of the constitution, like all paragraphs of all laws, serves not only to *include* certain particular "cases," but also to *exclude* other cases; for instance, the cases of those who are classified as "merely" economic refugees.

Consider, for instance, the young Tuareg man in my most recent novel, *Go, Went, Gone*: the state-owned French company Areva mines uranium in Niger. In return, it makes payments to the government of Niger, but this money never finds its way to the Tuareg, those disconcertingly defiant nomadic people who have lived traditionally for thousands of years in the region now claimed for mining. The extraction of uranium from the cliffs requires a great deal of water, which causes the water level to drop. Areva has even cut off Tuareg access to some watering holes entirely. Radioactive waste pollutes the ground. This has consequences for the camel herds on which the Tuareg depend for their livelihood; but it has even greater consequences for the Tuareg themselves. The rate of cancer and premature death for people in these regions is strikingly high. The energy produced in French atomic power plants from uranium mined in Niger continues to flow in France and Germany. But where is the freedom for one of these nomads to leave his country and seek his livelihood somewhere else, like France or Germany? Is a person in this situation really an "economic refugee"? Isn't he a political refugee after all? To say nothing of the destruction of age-old structures by these European corporations, social structures that have governed the lives of these people in their native countries for millennia, to say nothing of the moral and social vacuum that this destruction leaves behind, or of the violence and terror that flourish in this vacuum. To say nothing, even, of the consequences all this will have for future generations: the forced surrender of traditions, the loss of hope, the loss of autonomy, and of control over one's own existence.

Last fall, when I visited Princeton for a reading, I met a professor who proudly mentioned that she had urged one of Angela Merkel's advisors to accept Syrian refugees. But her advice was not that Germany should accept the refugees instead of rejecting them; rather, it was that if Germany had to accept refugees at all, then at least it should accept Syrian refugees instead of others who were less well educated and sophisticated. And they had to act fast before other countries beat them to the punch. She told Merkel's advisor that Syrians were elite as far as refugees were concerned; they'd be the easiest to integrate and the quickest to pay back into the system. That way Germany wouldn't have to accept those poor suckers, you know, the ones from the "shitholes"—like Niger, for example.

We saw the deal that Erdoğan and Merkel negotiated in 2016: For every illegal refugee who was sent back from Greece to Turkey, Germany would accept one legal refugee who was entitled to asylum. But after the deal was made, we saw how Erdoğan kept the educated, upper-class Syrian refugees in Turkey and only sent the old and infirm refugees to Germany. This distinction between life that is worth something and life that is worth nothing is a distinction that was made under Hitler, too. And it remains a matter of life and death, even if that may not be apparent at first sight. Survival is not just about the moment when someone is pulled from an overcrowded refugee boat, the moment when someone scales a fence. In the modern world of passports, quotas, emergency shelters, and exploitative black-market labor, survival is an ongoing, drawn-out process so painful that many people cannot endure it.

One of the refugees I spoke with for my last book suffered a mental breakdown after years of wandering around Europe without being allowed to work—a long odyssey that apparently included incidents of violence and abuse. He is now institutionalized in an Italian mental hospital, where he will probably remain forever.

Another, who had been granted temporary papers and a small apartment in Berlin on account of his serious heart problems, suffered a heart attack and died in that same apartment after barely a year. As I write in my most recent book, his father had been killed 15 years earlier in religious unrest in Nigeria, and his own two small children died in 2011 when the boat that was meant to carry them to safety in Europe capsized. After his death, it was discovered that in spite of his serious illness, he had been housing eight other people in his one-and-a-half-room flat, including a family of four with two small children. After years in emergency shelters, he was happy to finally have his own apartment, where he could offer help to friends who didn't know where else to turn.

When I went to the Muslim funeral home after his death, I learned that Syrian refugees often break down and die in the very moment when their families are allowed to join them—simply because the worry and the psychological strain on the refugees in Germany are so great. When this pressure is finally lifted, when the tension begins to loosen, their hold on their own lives loosens as well, with fatal consequences. The funeral home employee then added, without a trace of cynicism, that once the applicant has passed away, of course the family's immigration authorization is revoked.

While I was serving as volunteer legal guardian for one young refugee, another boy who lived in the same home for underage refugees—a 16-year-old Afghan boy—jumped to his death from a fourth-floor window.

A friend of mine has been caring for another teenage boy for two years; the boy recently learned that his mother had died in Afghanistan. Since then, he hardly ever leaves his room; he just lies in bed under the covers and doesn't go to school. While his classmates learn about mathematical constructs, English grammar, and nineteenth-century art history, this boy asks himself what will happen to his younger brother, whom their mother had been caring for. He asks himself if he failed as a son.

We hear stories like these, from this parallel world, from these blind spots in the happier world that we seem to see around us—if only we are willing to look and listen.

But are we willing?

Listening is an art—it is a risk—because those blind spots hide our own guilt and impotence. Even things that go wrong in other people's lives make us begin to fear for our own because it means that misfortune as such has not yet been cast out of our universe, and it may be infectious. What if there are problems that even money can't solve? We fear what can't be solved; we fear the gap that yawns between two sentences.

I am not a refugee, but my past also took place in a different country, and it was a stroke of good fortune that the Federal Republic simply issued us new West German passports—something refugees today can only dream of. But if someone like me, a privileged person who reaped the benefits of this transition, insists on speaking not only of benefits, but also of costs, are you willing to listen? If I say that despite all the comforts that I enjoy today, there is still a trace of sadness that cannot be effaced by the gains—how do you respond? Do you ask what that could be? Can you imagine that even in a country that is almost never spoken of without the qualifying phrase "rogue regime," someone could have had a happy childhood? Or that a number of my friends and I felt, when the reunification came, that history was simply sliding backward instead of moving forward? It is exhausting to think about these things, and to speak about them, just as it is to hear about them—just as it always is when things can't be easily separated into black and white. A language is more than a code.

The German Democratic Republic, as you all know, was that country with the wall, where everyone spied on everyone else, where the factories that had been the property of the East German people for forty years were left in a ramshackle condition, where all the streets were decked out in banners boasting ridiculous slogans. What else is there to say about that miniature Germany? The answer to this question is a deafening silence that grows louder from decade to decade. Is memory an instrument of power? Probably. How far do you have to step back in order to see an entire historical tapestry extending far beyond your own lifetime? How much do you have to know in order to understand what it really is that's flourishing in your own blind spot?

As a writer, I can take some satisfaction in the fact that I experienced such an upheaval, that I felt what it's like when a system that seems prepared to last for all eternity, through good times and bad, is suddenly wiped out in a matter of weeks. "Things will not stay as they are," Brecht wrote in a poem, and in that poem his sentence resounded with hope. Of course it can also be understood as a terrifying prophecy. And it seems to me that we only experience its truth when we learn to endure both gains and losses, which are often inseparably intertwined. When the wall fell, many East Germans ran straight into the arms of the new, the unknown. They ran with open arms to greet this new era, not knowing that its arrival would mark them forever as second-class citizens.

I remember a scene that occurred shortly after the fall of the wall, a few weeks before Christmas. In the dark of a December evening, a truck with a West Berlin license plate was parked on a muddy lot near the border crossing. From the tailgate of the truck, a West German, apparently the owner of a paper store, was handing out Christmas-themed wrapping paper to us East Germans, so that we, the needy people who didn't have such lovely, shiny wrapping paper, could have a chance to enjoy something pretty for a change. I'm sure that he meant well, he wanted to help.

The young woman who hurried past that scene as quickly as she could was in the blind spot of his consciousness. I was twenty-two at the time.

For me, his gesture as he handed down those rolls of paper from the tailgate embodied the whole misery of our inequality; it was a gesture of objective arrogance, so to speak. Most of all, it carried the message: I am above, and you are below. I come from another world, and I will only be here for a little while. This zone is contaminated, I'd rather not even set foot in it. I'm the one who can afford to give gifts. The present time that I live in is beautiful, shiny; it is already the future. Whereas the present time that these people live in, the needy people reaching for the wonderful wrapping paper, is just now turning into a "past present," that is to say, a past, which might best be left behind in that winter darkness, trampled into the mud. It's no accident that official usage since 1990 has referred to the "territory of the former German Democratic Republic" or to "former GDR citizens." Linguists ought to examine whether this designation makes any sense at all.

In retrospect, by the way, it seems particularly telling that the gift handed out by the generous paper seller was wrapping paper. Right after the fall of the wall, I started collecting East German packaging; I hung some samples on the wall of our Berlin apartment. They were made of rough, acidic paper, and they've faded so much from the sunlight that you can barely read the print: *Good buy—glad buy!* Or: *That's where I shop!* As if every shopper were a child. You can tell from the packaging that buying and selling didn't mean much in that country. The gray, gray East. Have you ever imagined Times Square without advertising? We reused our Christmas paper again and again, year after year. We kept our favorite paper in the family; after we exchanged gifts, my mother would fold it up and put it away in a basket, where it would stay until the following year. The practice of writing names on the wrapping paper was frowned upon, as was the use of tape, which might damage the paper when the gifts were unwrapped.

Of course, the nice paper seller who bent down to us from the tailgate couldn't have known any of that. And he didn't need to, either, since it wasn't long before the West German mark was introduced and we started buying that shiny wrapping paper for ourselves. We painted our houses in new, up-to-date colors, the fashion models from the East had their teeth straightened (even though no one had noticed before that they were slightly crooked), and the radio station suddenly decided that my voice was too high for me to read the book reviews I had written on the air, and hired someone else to read them instead. All of these changes served the same purpose, creating a new image that disguised the realities, giving the former East a face-lift. It was a complex transition to a world where things looked pretty and healthy, sounded good and wholesome, a transition to a world of pleasant aromas and smooth objects that fit comfortably in your hand: in other words, a world of things that were easy to sell, things that people were eager to buy. Whatever was broken, whatever was flawed, was left in the blind spots, in the shadows.

Recently, the minister of education of one of the East German states proposed a student exchange program between eastern and western Germany. The rationale was that the two parts of our country are still so different, so foreign to each other, that something must be done to improve their mutual understanding. A similar rationale could be given for a school exchange in this country between Manhattan and Mississippi, between Boise and Detroit, or just between a public and a private school in the same city.

A three-month exchange in your own country, even in your own city? Why not? Or to put it differently: Why? Why should someone who's doing just fine want to know what's happening in the blind spot of his consciousness? When someone with power does something for someone who is powerless, doesn't everything, even his interest itself, turn into a sort of handout? Is it possible, in the end, to take a vacation from the good fortune of one's own birth, just for three months? Just as a test, to broaden one's horizons—and then to quickly retreat into one's own skin? Or is a visit like that really the only chance that a privileged person has to experience what it is like to live in a world that he doesn't know and will never really know? And then? Is that an exchange—or tourism? Should we side with the Communists, who say that a well-meaning gift, or in this case the "well-meaning interest," only shores up the inequality of the system and is thus the opposite of empathy?

Or is it more than a handout when an individual takes it upon himself, for example, to enable another individual to live an independent life? We know the stories of Jewish people who only survived German fascism thanks to the brave decisions of individual helpers who offered them illegal aid. Surely it makes a difference whether a person survives—or not. And not only for that one person but also for the people close to him—friends, parents, also for his or her children who may one day come into the world, the grandchildren who may follow.

Shouldn't we always remember that we are all survivors in historical terms? The offspring of wars, massacres, natural disasters, misery—thanks to countless lucky accidents that saved the lives of our ancestors, thanks to numerous insurrections and revolutions, upheavals and new beginnings, thanks to helping hands like these, one in this century, one in another? How can we slip out of these two roles that world history has assigned us: victim and perpetrator? Or do the roles reverse of their own accord, and then reverse again and again? And if we happen to find ourselves among the better-off for the time being, do we buy an apartment? Where is the line that divides "us" from what is "foreign," what is "other"? Why is it just as difficult to get along with what is foreign, with what is other, as it is to get along without it? How well do you know your kidney? How well do you know your femur? Not well, I hope—but are they foreign to you? For the viruses and bacteria that live inside our bodies, the space within our skin is an entire planet. Orders of magnitude are always important, also. Or is the real point something else entirely? Who are we, that we may enjoy happiness at the expense of others thanks to a simple matter of selection? How long is the ramp from Auschwitz, anyway—and is it made of time? Perhaps it still hasn't come to an end? Selection . . .

These are not rhetorical questions. These are questions that

I ask myself. This country, for example, which was a place of refuge for the poor and the lost of Europe, still suffers today from the massive violence that was inflicted upon the indigenous Americans and upon the "slaves" imported from Africa. This country wants to show the whole world the happy ending of history, and yet it fails to arrive at an understanding even within its own borders, as we've seen day after day for 150 years. But we also see that attempts to repress this problem increasingly end in failure. And this failure expresses itself in violence. Yes, the word "freedom" sounds beautiful. But "equal rights" sounds beautiful as well.

And yet: Can we even afford equal rights? After all, we live on a planet in the middle of an unfathomable cosmos, on this lone planet with its limited resources. "The last war will be fought for the air we breathe," the wonderful German dramatist Heiner Müller once wrote. Yes, it's true, the resources are limited. But it's also true that 90 percent of the world's wealth is in the hands of 10 percent of the world's population. Or to say it once again, to put it clearly: 90 percent of the world's population is forced to share only 10 percent of the world's wealth. And even within this ridiculous 10 percent there is a hierarchy that drops off sharply. From physics and chemistry we know that gradients tend toward equilibrium. Have we forgotten that victories are always only temporary? Any expansion in the wake of victory is always expansion on the territory of the defeated, and that is always unfamiliar territory. The arrogance of the victor impedes cognition; that is the victor's greatest weakness, all human consequences aside.

We are now several thousand years into the history of education, and yet a professor at an elite university in this country can still imagine no other criterion, no other possible basis for a person's social acceptance, aside from sheer *usefulness*. The human being is degraded to a sort of raw material. To be sure, this attitude might resonate in a society structured around the maximization of profit. But human beings, thank God, are not machines that can be turned on and off at will. You and I don't want to be slaves, but slaves, of course, do not want to be slaves either. The experiences, memories, hopes, traumas, griefs, and joys of all people, including the disregarded and discarded, spread their branches far and wide, across places and times, obeying rules that we barely know. What appears from the perspective of Europe or North America to be nothing but a blind spot is, in fact, an entire world, whether we look at it or not—even if these worlds are hidden behind walls, fences, in far-off camps, or in the bad neighborhood around the corner. An eight-meter-high fence is not a sign of strength but a sign of fear. A sign of the fear of being questioned. Fear of loss, poverty, and death. That is our fear, and it is no different from the fear of the people on the other side of the fence. For we were made from dust, and to dust we shall return. In other words: We, you and I, come from shitholes, too.

UNIVERSITY OF OKLAHOMA
MARCH 9, 2018